WTF?!

I HAVE CANCER?

How to Get Through the
Hardest Time of Your Life
With Strength and Optimism

LAREN RUSCH WATSON

BALBOA.
PRESS

A DIVISION OF HAY HOUSE

Balboa Press books may be ordered through booksellers or by contacting:

Balboa Press
A Division of Hay House
1663 Liberty Drive
Bloomington, IN 47403
www.balboapress.com
1 (877) 407-4847

Because of the dynamic nature of the Internet, any web addresses or links contained in this book may have changed since publication and may no longer be valid. The views expressed in this work are solely those of the author and do not necessarily reflect the views of the publisher, and the publisher hereby disclaims any responsibility for them.

The author of this book does not dispense medical advice or prescribe the use of any technique as a form of treatment for physical, emotional, or medical problems without the advice of a physician, either directly or indirectly. The intent of the author is only to offer information of a general nature to help you in your quest for emotional and spiritual well-being. In the event you use any of the information in this book for yourself, which is your constitutional right, the author and the publisher assume no responsibility for your actions.

Any people depicted in stock imagery provided by Thinkstock are models, and such images are being used for illustrative purposes only. Certain stock imagery © Thinkstock.

Print information available on the last page.

ISBN: 978-1-5043-5334-2 (sc)
ISBN: 978-1-5043-5336-6 (hc)
ISBN: 978-1-5043-5335-9 (e)

Library of Congress Control Number: 2016905066

Balboa Press rev. date: 05/03/2016

While writing this book, I lost my dear brother Jeff to a similarly random and weird cancer diagnosis. His was lung cancer, although he never smoked a day in his life. By the time it was diagnosed, it had metastasized to his bones and brain. I flew down to his home and shared the ideas of this book with him, and he took them on with gusto. I know they helped him find some balance at a really challenging time. I miss him dearly and dedicate this book to him.

TABLE OF CONTENTS

INTRODUCTION

I have had many labels: graphic designer, wife, mother, foodie, nutritionist, health coach, blogger, yogi. None of them prepared me for the most challenging label of them all: double whammy cancer patient.

This book is about my cancer journey and what I learned along the way. Some of it was deep and life-altering; some of it was uplifting and healing. As a health coach who was already taking very good care of her body, the diagnoses of two aggressive, life-threatening, and hard to treat cancers at essentially the same time was shocking. Throughout the two-year physical and emotional roller coaster that was my life, I learned to let go, forgive, receive, find balance, and tune in. There were trippy personalized messages from the Universe and big perspective changers (there is nothing like cancer hitting you upside the head to put life in perspective). This book is for people who have recently been diagnosed with cancer and are in the sea of overwhelm about it all, and for people who know someone with cancer and want to know how best to support them.

Getting a cancer diagnosis can derail you in the most fundamental ways. You feel lost, hopeless, confused, angry, and *scared*. I felt all of those things big time. Some things that I did right off the bat set me up for success in the treatment that followed. Other things I learned along the way. Some lessons came up over and over, and I had to keep relearning them. Many of the adjustments I made were mental; some of them were physical. And to tell you the truth, the mental adjustments were at least as important as anything I did to prepare myself physically.

Because I was a health coach and already eating foods full of antioxidants and avoiding inflammatory processed, pesticide-laden food, I felt that I had that part under control. For me, I didn't think the cancers were about the food I was eating or a lack of exercise. For other people, those may be big factors. Or someone might have a satisfying spiritual practice, but his or her area of neglect is in food or exercise.

I knew if I was going to do any work on myself that might help remove the cancer permanently, it was going to be soul work. I needed to delve into the spiritual side. I began meditating, visualizing, journaling, and forgiving. I started looking at my "perfectionist tendencies" to see if they really served me. I had profound insights that I will share in the following pages.

But if your area of need isn't in the spiritual arena, and you suspect it has to do with food, you may be right. Research shows that cancer has a lot to do with the food. In reference to the link between diet and cancer, the National Institutes of Health says that "up to a third of deaths may be linked to lifestyle factors such as diet, physical activity, and obesity"[1]. Are you wondering about pesticides on your food perhaps being part of how you got cancer? Studies have shown that many pesticides are carcinogenic,[2] and other chemicals, such as those in the plastics our food is packaged in, are endocrine disruptors that have been linked to cancer.[3] We are exposed to literally thousands of chemicals on a daily basis, the vast majority of which have never been tested in human studies.

Part 2 of this book has suggestions related to food and lifestyle changes to consider for anyone diagnosed with cancer, or really for anyone wanting to be healthier. Eating healthfully and avoiding chemicals keep our immune systems strong and able to fight off disease. I suspect there were foods I was intolerant to that I ate for years that actually negatively affected my immune system, possibly creating an environment that was easier for the cancer cells to grow. One thing I know is that it is possible to eat and live in such a way that helps your immune system do its job of seeking out and killing the random abnormal cancerous cells most people have in their bodies from the modern world in which we live.

I have divided this book into two parts: the *what* and the *how*—what happened to me and how I got through it. Part 1 is my story—all the hell and the hard work I did to survive a double cancer diagnosis as well as what I learned along the way. Part 2, how I got through it, goes deeper into the lessons I learned and what a person with cancer might consider doing to help the process be easier (all good practices for the noncancer patient as well) physically, mentally, and spiritually. I have divided how I got through it into seven categories, full of practical advice about what to eat, how to best set your body up for healing, how to win the mental game, how to deal with the fear and worry, how to accept what is happening, and the importance of finding quiet time to go within.

Whether you are a cancer patient, have a loved one who is a cancer patient, are a patient with another serious diagnosis, or simply someone who would like to avoid this terrible experience, my hope is that you benefit from my story and that my experience helps you in your journey toward long-term health and wellness.

Part 1

WHAT HAPPENED TO ME

1

A LITTLE BUMP

I am really late to my kids' swim meet. It is late July, and these are the semifinals, called Southern Division in our area. The place is packed and loud and chaotic, with swimmers hustling to the blocks and parents shouting from the sidelines. I find my friends on the metal stands the pool has brought in for the event and slip in next to my friend Ashley, who has graciously saved me a seat in prime viewing real estate. She is one of the few people with whom I've shared what has been going on. Another friend turns and asks why I'm so late. "I had a doctor's appointment," I reply. She asks jokingly, "What, are you sick?" smiling, knowing this is highly unlikely. I'm the healthiest person she knows—a health coach, in great shape, and drinking my green smoothies every day. I say, "I might be, but I don't want to talk about it," tears welling in my eyes. I look away and try to distract myself with the meet. She texts me "I'm sorry" from two seats away. I am sorry too. The whole thing is so totally, completely unbelievable.

That day I had just come from the ear, nose and throat doctor. He had said that the little bump on the side of my neck was probably lymphoma. The whole drive to the meet, I had been busy convincing myself that he didn't know what he was talking about. That was impossible. I was a health coach! I had just had a checkup and had perfect cholesterol numbers and everything! Little did I know that not only was he right that it was lymphoma but I would find out a year later that I also had breast cancer at the same time. Yes, two separate and distinct cancers, and both aggressive, rare, and hard to treat, at the same time.

It all started in June of 2013. I was having lunch with girlfriends when I noticed a little bump on the side of my neck. It was my friend Jana's birthday, and four of us were at a local bar/restaurant celebrating. As the lunch was winding down, and Ashley had run off back to work, I just happened to put my hand right on the little pebble-sized bump on the side of my neck while I was talking. It was like my body was telling me, "Hey, check this out. Something's not right here." I said to my friends Jana and Paula, who were sitting across the table, "This is weird. I have a bump on my neck." A few days later, I showed it to my chiropractor, and he said it was a swollen lymph node and suggested massaging it to clear whatever it was trying to detox. I did that for a week, but nothing changed. When I got two more bumps after a bit-too-boozy Fourth of July, I called my naturopathic doctor. When I confessed that my Google search of "lump on neck" came up with lymphoma, she said she was sure it was easily explained, a viral or fungal infection perhaps. "But maybe we should get a biopsy to rule out the worst scenario just so you can stop worrying about it. I'll consult with an oncologist colleague." Next thing I knew, my life was upside down.

Two words you never want to hear from any doctor: "biopsy" and "oncologist." I tried so hard not to be scared. But this was very, very scary. The larger of the two that had popped up after the Fourth of July was chosen for the biopsy. This was my first-ever surgery and first-ever general anesthesia. I was so scared I cried at the hospital. Is there anything not scary about anesthesia? Your life is completely in someone else's hands (the '70s movie *Coma* had made a big impression on me). My surgeon and anesthesiologist thankfully did a beautiful job and the surgeon even managed to put the incision in one of the already existing lines in my neck. At the follow-up appointment for the surgery, I asked him how noticeable the scar would be. He said, "That's the least of your concerns." As it turns out, for a roughly three-inch scar, it's not nearly as noticeable as it could have been, and my vanity thanks him for that.

Off the biopsy went to the lab, and let me tell you, the two days it takes to get the results back are the longest two days of your life. The pathology came back, and the lymphoma was confirmed. Turns out that worst-case scenario that my naturopath had been reassuring me wasn't it, really was it. Only later I would find out it was worse than the worst-case scenario. The results from the lymph node in my neck showed B-cell non-Hodgkins lymphoma. My oncologist at first told me this "wasn't doom and gloom." It was easily treatable, and if you were going to get cancer, this was a good one to get. Even though I couldn't believe he would say such a thing, I was actually encouraged by this, while I let the shock sink in. He also said they would next need to do a bone marrow biopsy to see how pervasive the cancer was. Lymphoma is a blood disease, and blood is created in the bone marrow. This was not another surgery; it was a rather simple procedure they did right in one of the doctor's offices.

So an appointment for a bone marrow biopsy was made for the next day. All of these appointments happened within days of that day at the swim meet when I was barely keeping it together emotionally.

It was a whirlwind of doctor's appointments, which in a way helped distract me from the fear. There were places to go and people to see. However, the urgency with which they treated the situation was also scary. To me, their availability communicated a seriousness without actually using words. My case was clearly a priority. I mean, when do you ever hear from a doctor that they can get you later that same day?

The bone marrow biopsy needed no anesthesia, thankfully, just numbing at the site, and was performed in one of the oncologist's rooms with just him and one nurse. I was all numbed up, and all was going well until the doctor started turning the screw-like needle into my lower back at the hip bone to get a sample of the marrow. He had to push hard, and it felt kind of like (only opposite to) having a tooth pulled. It was at this crucial moment that my husband, who had been holding my hand for moral support and facing the doctor on the other side of the table, actually passed out in the middle of the procedure. "Man down!" the doctor shouts. (Seriously! I am not making this up.) "Get some nurses in here!" All attention turned to Ted, my husband. Even the doctor was telling them how to position him flat on the floor, not upright. I'm thinking, *Uh, could we finish this up? I've got a drill needle inside my hip bone over here.* It felt like I was in a Woody Allen movie. I actually started laughing. The down side was that the doctor said that in all the activity he hadn't gotten a good sample and would have to go in again. My husband won't be living that one down any time soon.

Again, I was waiting for biopsy results. The next day, the pathology of the bone marrow showed that not only was it most certainly lymphoma, it was mantle cell non-Hodgkins lymphoma, a rare type, and with the rate of onset, seemingly fast growing and aggressive. The look on my oncologist's face as he shared this bit of news was unsettling. The previous "this is not doom and gloom" encouragement was gone. This was serious.

The results also showed that this was a blood cancer that unfortunately had taken over 40 percent of my bone marrow. A PET scan three days later showed that no other organs were affected, thankfully, but once cancer is in your bone marrow, you are at stage 4. The odds were not in my favor.

The thing about having a blood cancer in your bone marrow (where all blood cells are born) is that you can't do surgery to get rid of it. And unlike what some people may have you believe, with mantle cell, you can't just eat turkey tail mushrooms or cannabis oil or go vegan to cure this one. Being the natural holistic health coach that I am, believe me, I would much rather have used a natural remedy and not done chemo. I believe those remedies can work on some cancers and have worked for some people. But with this kind of stage 4 aggressive mantle cell cancer, the kind that had invaded my blood and bone marrow in a matter of weeks, those natural remedies would not have been strong enough to save my life. It would have been like throwing gravel at a bear—not powerful enough to stop it. Even my naturopathic doctor said that I would have to hit the mantle cell hard and fast.

2

FEAR

L ots of books are written on fear—overcoming it or not letting it control you—and, to tell you the truth, I have read none of them. I am not saying that I haven't been afraid in my life, but, to be honest, I've had it pretty good. I haven't had any traumatic events— no serious emergency room visits, no life-threatening situations. Until this.

The concept that I may not survive this I could. Not. Be. With. It terrified me. I stuffed that fear way down. I basically went straight into denial that the biopsy results had indicated anything of the sort. I had switched to a superstar, famous, specialist in mantle cell lymphoma, and his team was running more tests. Maybe things were inconclusive. Unfortunately, in the end, they only confirmed what the first round had shown.

And with that confirmation, I lost the cap I had on my emotions. They all came tumbling out. The fear, the anger, the tears. Lots and lots of tears. Fear is an emotion that will not be suppressed for long. It demands to be felt. When you feel it, experience it, it subsides. Bravery can then step in. I rode the fear—bravery rollercoaster all throughout this experience. It never really went away. But it became manageable.

When the diagnosis came back and I fell apart, I didn't want to scare my children so I managed to hold it together and cry when they weren't around. And I wondered how could this possibly be happening? I didn't want to die. At least, not any time soon. I had always assumed I would live into my nineties like the women typically have done in my family.

I had to tell the kids. I'm not sure if this was the right thing to do, but when I told them that I had cancer, it was called mantle cell lymphoma, and that I had the best doctor, I was going to get treatment, and it would all be over by Christmas. I told them that I wasn't going to die. I told them that the treatment would be rough, but I was strong, and it would all be okay in the end. Neither of them said much but seemed reassured by my story. My daughter cried a little, probably a little more in tune with my own fear. The treatment was going to start the day after their first day of school. Each was starting in a new school that year (high school and middle school), and to this day, I feel terrible that I wasn't more available for that transition. But I couldn't. My treatment would require five-day stays in the hospital under continuous chemotherapy.

3

THE PROTOCOL

With the news that I had a rare and hard to treat form of non-Hodgkins lymphoma, my husband asked my oncologist at the time who the best doctor to treat mantle cell was. He kindly referred us to a world-renowned oncologist at Seattle Cancer Care Alliance, a facility people fly in from all over the world to go to for this kind of cancer, and, as luck would have it, was in Seattle, where we live. With some pestering, we got an appointment with this superstar doctor and switched my care to him.

At our first appointment, he told me that there is no cure for mantle cell and that permanent remission was my best hope. I will never forget this appointment. He talked quickly and in a friendly but extremely knowledgeable way about B cells and T cells, the immune system, and the lymph system. He told me how with me one B cell at some point had split funny and the #14 chromosome got stuck on the #11 chromosome, and that there's a part of the 11 on the 14. By the time they can detect mantle cell, it has usually spread throughout the lymph system and into the bone marrow and organs and is usually at stage 4 before detected. It is a rare lymphoma, found in only 6 percent of the lymphomas, and is more common in men over sixty-five. That certainly didn't describe me. He then presented me with three treatment options, each harsher than the previous one. They all included induction chemotherapy to get to remission for phase 1 with differing phase 2 options. He explained that they would all get me to remission, and the difference was if they would keep me in remission.

Option 1: Retuxan and Bendamustine, a mild regimen of a few hours of chemo each time, and I wouldn't even lose my hair.

Option 2: R-CHOP (acronym for a particular chemical cocktail), more toxic than Retuxan/Bendamustine. But with nearly all patients in this option and the Retuxan/Bendamustine option, the disease will come back within three to five years without a postremission management plan.

Option 3: Hyper-CVAD, the most difficult regimen, requiring four hospital stays, each of five days in length on continuous drip, with twenty-one days between treatments. This was harsh but this option offered complete remissions in 90 percent of the patients.

Next in the discussion came my options for the postremission management. This was all written on a white board in two columns, and I felt like I could pick and choose an induction chemotherapy plan from column A with a postremission plan from column B. Kind of like the chemical version of lunch specials at some kind of chemo restaurant. "I would like toxic chemical combo platter number 1 with a number 2 side of indefinite chemo, please."

Post Remission Management:
Option 1: No treatment until the disease comes back (not recommended).

Option 2: Maintenance chemo of Retuxan, where I would take a dose of this drug every three months indefinitely.

Option 3: An autologous stem cell transplant. This is controversial, but he felt that it gave me the highest chance of remission for fifteen to twenty years. But the stem cell transplant had to be done right after the induction chemo for the best results.

After a few sleepless nights, some soul searching, and advice from friends and family, I chose option 3 in both cases, which on the chemo restaurant menu was the harsher than hell chemo with a stem cell transplant chaser. This would bring me to remission and give me a clean slate with the transplant. What I liked best was it would be bringing the big guns to the fight (even though I abhor guns and fighting) and gave me the best chance of meeting my grandchildren.

4

THE TREATMENT

Within a week, on September 5, the day after both my kids started at new schools, I checked into the UW Medical Center Hospital seventh-floor chemo ward to start the hyper-CVAD chemo protocol, which, as I mentioned earlier, required four five-day hospital stays on a twenty-one-day cycle. I had only ever stayed the night in a hospital when my two babies were born. And that was a posh brand new maternity ward. This was, well, not that. This was beeping chemo machines all night and staff waking me up at all hours to take my vitals. I hated it. It was impossible to get any sleep, and don't get me started on the food. I'm a health coach foodie who loves cooking tasty whole food nutrient-dense meals. So the hamburgers and milkshakes (certainly not) and farmed fish with boring steamed vegetables (not much better) were not anything I was going to eat.

Luckily, my friends saved me. My friend Heidi brought me a smoothie most mornings for breakfast, and if she didn't bring one, she arranged for another friend to deliver. She brought me funny movies to watch to keep my spirits up, and I had a lot of visitors to make the time pass. It was hard to be away from my kids and husband. Ted came to visit me every day, but the kids only came once each hospital stay. It was not easy for them to see me that way. We tried to make it fun by playing Scrabble, but I could tell it was hard on them. So Ted and I decided to limit that part of it for the kids. I tried to talk to them about how they were doing and how this was affecting them, but they were twelve and fourteen and not very adept at expressing their emotions. "It's okay" was about as much as I could get out of them. When I asked my son if he was worried, he asked, "Should I be?" I said, "No, everything's going to be okay." It was what I wanted them to believe. And who knew really?

The days in the hospital were spent reading and surfing the Internet for funny videos; YouTube snippets of Jimmy Fallon and Ellen DeGeneres sustained me. I realized I couldn't read books while in the hospital not only because of the steady stream of attending nurses but my attention couldn't be sustained that long. I could only focus on magazines, so friends brought all varieties from *Vanity Fair* and *Vogue* to *People*.

Hyper-CVAD is an acronym for four different chemotherapies. I thought they were going to mix them all together in a chemo cocktail, but they actually gave me them one at a time. As a result, fear took hold with each new kind of chemo, since I didn't know how my body would tolerate it. Turns out I tolerated them well and didn't have side effects, thankfully. In the end, each five-day stay in the hospital was utterly and completely boring! I couldn't wait to be released each time. I was nauseous and fatigued afterward, and it seemed to be cumulative with each treatment. But I had medications for the nausea that worked well. I was also seeing a naturopathic oncologist who was plying me with dozens of supplements tailored to the specific effects of the chemo I was getting to mitigate the side effects. I highly recommend having a naturopathic oncologist on your team. Mine was so caring and tender. She seemed to have endless time for me. In stark contrast to my other oncologist, she spent hours with me. I talked to her about all of my concerns. She offered support, suggestions, and supplements. I loved her.

5

MAJOR SOUL-SEARCHING

The four rounds of chemo for five days at the hospital each time may sound bad, and it wasn't great, but it was actually the days after the stem cell transplant that turned out to be the hardest and the weakest I have ever been in my life. After the transplant, I was slightly stronger than a puddle on the floor.

But can we go back to the days right after the diagnosis? The shock. The disbelief. I was a holistic health coach! I was drinking green smoothies. I was doing yoga and seasonal detox cleanses. How could I, of all people, get cancer? This shook me to my core. And perhaps the weirdest part was that I felt perfectly healthy. The doctors kept asking if I had felt any fatigue. Nope. Night sweats? I felt fine! It was so hard to believe this diagnosis was true. I kept waiting for someone to call and say there had been a mistake. How could this terrible thing be happening in my body when I felt completely normal?

I felt like I had to figure out this un-figure-out-able thing. It was very tempting to go down the self-blame path and think that I had done something wrong. I knew there was no cheese down that path, but I just couldn't help thinking there must have been more healthy living I could have done. More yoga? More meditation? Should I have trained for a marathon? What had I not been doing?

I have spent a lot of time thinking about this because I was so sure of myself and my healthy lifestyle. It was a betrayal of the highest order for me to get cancer when I had been doing everything the books said to do. And yet, despite all my smoothies, veggies, and yoga, this cancer had invaded and managed to spread. So I searched for the answer. What was I missing? I was healthy physically, but was I healthy emotionally, mentally, and spiritually? Was I happy, joyful, and brazenly loving life? I had to be honest with myself. I was happy most of the time. But blissfully, joyfully, and brazenly loving life? Not so much.

I'm a perfectionist by nature, and I began to realize that my high standards had gotten in the way of true happiness and peace of mind. I had been hard on my husband, hard on my kids, and, most of all, hard on myself. I stressed myself out trying to be the perfect wife, the perfect mother, and the perfect business person. I was not always easy to be around. I wanted to be happy and love life. I was just so busy trying to do everything perfectly that I wasn't fully enjoying the life I had.

I also realized that while taking care of everyone else, for the most part, I had put my own needs on the back burner. This is astonishingly common among the women I know. We are career women, mothers, and wives, working from the minute we wake up to the minute we drop exhausted on the bed at night, having taken care of everyone but ourselves. "Who has time for that?" I hear my friends say.

Making my self-care a priority had never been part of my mind-set. My mother put us kids first; she sacrificed for us. She ate the fried egg with the broken yolk that no one else wanted. I adore my mother, and she did not teach me to put my needs above those of my family. The idea that we women should make sure our needs are met, that our energy cup is full in order to have some to share, the idea to put our oxygen masks on first before helping others, was not part of my upbringing. Asking for help, or arranging things so I had time for self-care, was not what I was used to.

So with this diagnosis, since I really felt as if I knew what I was doing on the nutrition side of things, what I decided to do was dive into this other side of healthy living: self-care, the happiness factor, and stress reduction practices—the setting free of my spirit.

I started meditating in earnest. Twice a day! (As a perfectionist, I was going to do this right!) I went to a spiritual center on Sundays. I was not brought up with any religion and have always kind of made up my own spirituality. It's basically a combination of the Golden Rule and most of the Ten Commandments, with some reincarnation and returning to Love Source when you die, thrown in. I jumped into exploring this side of life with both feet. And amazingly to me, I actually had some trippy experiences when I started tuning in (more on this in part 2). Words that I knew were not my own came to me in the form of answers or replies. I was either going crazy, or I was becoming spiritual.

6

THANK YOU, CANCER!

One serendipitous thing that happened was that just when I wanted to make a daily practice of meditation, Oprah and Deepak Chopra launched a twenty-one-day meditation called Perfect Health. What a perfect topic! It began on the day that I met with the first oncologist who found I had enlarged lymph nodes in multiple places on my body.

The first meditation's centering thought was, "I am open to miracles." Boy, was I ever open to miracles that day! It was very helpful. On day twelve, the centering thought, which I repeated continuously as I went into my PET scan, just having drunk radioactive sugar water for the cancer to eat up and then glow for the camera, was, "I use my energy to heal and transform." I couldn't have thought of a more perfect phrase to repeat during that process.

These centering thoughts had all been spot-on, which was eerie and cool. The one that brought me to tears, though, was the one on gratitude. Oprah started the meditation by saying that "having appreciation for whatever shows up in your life actually recalibrates your very vibration." I thought to myself, *Appreciation for whatever shows up in my life? Like this cancer? How in the hell do I have appreciation for cancer showing up in my life? Is that even possible?*

But I took this concept on during the rest of the meditation. I searched for ways to thank cancer for showing up. Tears rolled down my face as what I found was twofold: that this cancer had already benefited my life in several ways, and that this attitude of gratitude was much more peaceful and positive than my previous attitude of bitter resentment toward the cancer.

What happened when I was diagnosed with mantle cell lymphoma was that my friends showed up. And when I say they showed up, I mean *showed up*. I really have the best friends in the world. They rallied to my side unflinchingly and created a huge web of support in very short order. They arranged food for me at the hospital (because it was horrible, sorry to say). They took over child care and rides to and from school. They delivered meals for my family's dinner when I was in the hospital as well as when I was home recovering. They offered to clean my house. They sent cards and flowers and hats and scarves when I went bald. I was and continue to be incredibly grateful for it all. The outpouring of love was amazing and beautiful, and I so appreciated it. It was actually uncomfortable for me and hard to receive at first. But I knew I should just let it in.

The second thought from the meditation was that this cancer had already given me valuable perspective about what is truly important in life. Success, proving yourself, perfection, and being right are definitely not it. Peace, love, kindness, laughing, joy, and spending time with loved ones is what it's all about. I don't really think

I was extreme in this regard before this cancer came along, but I did have my overachiever perfectionist tendencies as previously mentioned, and I saw that I had lost perspective as I impatiently built my new health coaching business. Having more positive thoughts and lowering my stress levels were two areas that I saw need for improvement.

7

BEING BALD

So having made it through all of the chemo really well with the help of my naturopathic oncologist, and because I went in very healthy otherwise (glad for my years of eating kale and broccoli), my main objective was to regain my strength after the chemo. I walked, and eventually I got stronger. And then in November, I was declared in remission. (Yay! They should really hand out gold leaf certificates!)

But I had lost my hair—all of it. Every hair on my body except thankfully some of my eyebrows. This was something I was dreading and was having a lot of trouble accepting. When I first got the news that I might need chemo, what concerned me most was losing my hair. Of course, I didn't like the idea of poison coursing through my veins killing off my immune system (that I had ironically worked hard to get strong over the last few years since my dairy allergy diagnosis). No, the one aspect of chemo that brought me literally to tears every time I thought about it was the idea of losing my hair.

I had been warned by a cancer survivor that as soon as you're bald, your secret becomes public, and that is exactly how I felt. Before your hair falls out, you can walk around and, especially if you're having very few symptoms from your cancer or treatment, act like a normal person, and no one is the wiser. But as soon as the hair is gone, *everybody knows*. It is a huge public statement that I just didn't want to make. I didn't want people to see me as a sick person.

Besides, I really liked my hair. I have played a lot with it over the years—short, long, curly, straight, even asymmetrical in college. I've always felt that you could tell a lot about a person by his or her haircut. So now my lack of hair said something about me. It said "cancer patient." This was hard to be with. Of course, I knew that I could wear a wig, but I was afraid people would be able to tell it was a wig. And I considered what a wig communicates: "Cancer patient who doesn't want the world to know" perhaps? I didn't really care if people knew, I was blogging about it after all. I just really didn't want to be a cancer patient.

I had heard of a man in Bellevue who could make a wig from your own hair in your own hairstyle. I decided to give that a go. Maybe I could pull that off. And there were always hats. I would need to make sure I had some amazing earrings. It began to feel like I could survive going bald. It may sound vain, but going bald was really hard for me. I learned there are multiple levels of bravery to this cancer thing. And there's certainly nothing easy or fun about it. But I was determined to make it through. What else could I do?

So as soon as my hair started falling out, which was eleven days from the first chemo treatment, I dashed to the wonderful man in Bellevue who makes wigs for cancer patients. He cut my hair off to the scalp in a very strategic way, placing the pieces on boards, essentially mapping out my head and my hairstyle. He took measurements of my skull. *The next day* it was ready. He had sewn all of the pieces of hair onto a piece of silk that he then got wet and formed to my head. Unfortunately the hair got wet in the process, and he had to restyle the fresh blow out and flat-iron job I had done to my naturally curly hair the day before. I asked if this new wig would be like my old hair and get frizzy in the rain, or if the blow out would stay. He said, "It's your hair. It will do what your hair did." Weird!

So after picking it up, I wore it to a nearby mall with my girlfriend Ashley and proceeded to freak out. I imagined everyone was looking at it trying to figure out if my hair was real. I was in a clothing store, and a man my age smiled at me. I assumed he could tell I was wearing a wig and was a cancer patient, and was smiling because he felt sorry for me. I lasted about an hour and had to go home. Even though it was a gorgeous wig and fit my head perfectly and was rather expensive, I only ended up wearing it a half dozen times.

I live in a suburb of Seattle and know a lot of the locals. I *always* see someone I know in the grocery store. And since I had been pretty public blogging about my condition and the emotional upheaval of it all, if I wore the wig in town, I got questions because people knew I was really bald. It may seem strange, but wearing the wig felt fake and inauthentic. So I wore it to Seattle or to any large event where I wanted to be anonymous and not have people see me as a cancer patient. But the baldness, and the stigma, still bothered me. I wanted to be authentic, but I wasn't badass enough (yet) to walk around bald.

I decided to turn to hats. This worked well because it was fall and then winter, and I could easily wear a big warm hat, and no one would really notice I was bald underneath. I absolutely needed something on my head because I quickly found out being bald is cold! I immediately felt sorry for all the bald men in the world and how they must need to be constantly regulating the temperature of their heads. Luckily, I found I look good in hats. I collected a large assortment of colors and fashion styles, many given to me by sweet, generous friends. I also collected scarves for my neck. I never realized how insulating my long hair was! Accessories were my new friend.

Before a Christmas party, I got wild and crazy and bought a bright blue wig. I thought it would be fun—kind of Katy Perry-ish. The blue wig was obviously fake, and for some reason that made it easier for me to wear.

8

GRAY IS THE NEW BLACK

As my hair grew back that first time, I got to see how much of it was gray! I had been coloring my hair brown since my midthirties. I highlighted it in my twenties until my hair stylist said there was too much gray, and we needed to switch to allover color. I went with a very natural dark brown permanent hair color and dyed it religiously every four to five weeks for the next ten years. I have since found out that there is a chemical in brown and black hair dye that has been linked to non-Hodgkins lymphoma! People who color their hair have a 50 percent higher chance of getting non-Hodgkins lymphoma and are three times as likely to get breast cancer (not to mention other cancers, such as bladder, ovarian, and more). The two cancers that I got![4] Hmm. That chemical should really be banned, don't you think?

As my hair grew back in, I decided to let it be its natural grayish very dark brown, almost black color. Let's call it salt and pepper. This was a big adjustment for me because not only was I wrestling with being a cancer patient, then survivor, not weak but strong! I now had to look in the mirror and see someone who looked like a grandma at the age of forty eight. Not that there's anything wrong with grandmas. I just wasn't one yet and wanted to look younger. I played around a lot with spiking gels and flatirons to give me a more youthful version of salt and pepper.

Being Bald Again … And Again

Slowly my gray hair grew back in, and got to about two inches long, only to have it all fall out again after the stem cell transplant. After the transplant, it took about three months to have half an inch in length and about six months before it was a good inch long. I would end up losing it a third time after the breast cancer diagnosis. By then I was used to it and barely gave a thought to going out in public with a bald head. "It is what it is" was my motto by then.

The third time I went bald, after my mastectomy, I had gotten a decent length going in my attempt to have long hair again. It was perhaps 4 inches long when it started falling out from the breast cancer chemotherapy. Since this time I wasn't going to have a wig made out of my hair, I decided to see how long I could maintain some semblance of hair on my head. I let it dry naturally curly because messing with it too much left a lot of hair in my hands and in the sink. I have thick hair to begin with, so this slow, gradual process lasted for longer than you might think. It was a kind of slow torture. I began pulling it back off my head in one of my daughter's thin headbands. People said it looked cute. I wanted to believe them. I thought maybe I was actually pulling this off until I went to my brother's memorial service.

Yes, if you read the dedication of this book, you read that my brother Jeff died of lung cancer in the middle of my two cancer diagnoses. So horrible and tragic and sad, and his friends, my other brother, sister, and my mother actually managed to create a beautiful memorial service in the midst of all of our grief. So what happened with my hair at my brother's service was that I hugged one of his dear friends who is tall and had one of those scruffy super short beards just longer than a five o'clock shadow. As I pulled away from the hug, I noticed a big chunk of my hair had stuck to his cheek. I smiled and removed it, without explaining. What's a cancer patient to do?

It was shortly after the hair-on-cheek incident that my husband mentioned that my hair was getting a bit "patchy" in the back. The back? I hadn't even looked at the back. We got out the buzzers and shaved my head the next day. I was sad all over again. But I was also pretty used to it by now. I had much more of a well-adjusted attitude toward it. "It is what it is." I do know that I was much less concerned that time around about what people thought of my bald head. That time it was summer, and, yes, I wore all sorts of sun hats, but I also brazenly went baldheaded out into the world, with my aviator sunglasses and flat-chested sundresses.

9

FIVE MILLION STEM CELLS

So with the remission declaration following my four rounds of heavy-duty chemo, I had to get my bald self ready for the stem cell transplant in about a month. Before they would do the transplant, they checked every system and organ in my body to make sure it was up to this monumental endeavor. They checked my heart with an hour long echocardiogram. They checked my lungs with a very interesting lung capacity breath analyzer that resembled the Cone of Silence on *Get Smart*. They even checked my teeth. I passed all checks and was relieved to know my body was in good shape.

If you don't know what a stem cell transplant is, join the club. I certainly didn't before all of this. Stem cells are created in the bone marrow and are your body's brand new baby cells. The amazing thing about stem cells is that they can turn into any kind of cell that the body needs. For a transplant, basically the idea is to wipe out the immune system and give it a do-over. You get even harsher chemo or radiation, wiping out all of your white blood cells (a.k.a. your immune system). Then they give you back, in my case, my own previously harvested stem cells to grow brand new white blood cells to re-create the immune system.

The doctors needed to harvest five million of these puppies to do my stem cell transplant. For me this was done between the third and fourth hyper-CVAD treatments. It took three four-hour sessions in Apheresis, the amazing process where a machine looped my blood through tubes and spun out the stem cells, returning the rest of the blood back into me. On the first day, the nurse said to me, "You're so young and healthy; they'll get all five million in the first try!" Well, they got 1.5 million. The process was painless but left me worn out. And I had to go back the next day to try for more. I talked to my bone marrow as I tried to fall asleep that night. I told the stem cells to rally and multiply because they needed to do an important job. I fell asleep confident that the next day they would get the 3.5 million they needed. Well, they got another 1.5 million.

I was crushed. I'll never forget that day because it was Halloween. My daughter and her friends were going out in the neighborhood, and it's a party not only for the kids but for the adults where we live. I was really looking forward to doing this fun evening and just feeling normal. I could even wear my fun blue wig, and no one would think twice. I had missed all of my daughter's basketball games from fatigue and/or low immune function, and I so wanted to participate in Halloween just to feel normal. I told the nurse when she called to tell me they had only gotten 1.5 million more, that coming in to the hospital tonight "didn't work for me." As if I had any say in the matter. The nurse told me rather sternly, "You need to come in tonight and harvest more. We are trying to save your life." And that was that—it was another exercise of many in letting go. I went in, and they got what they needed that night.

10

THE BIG KAHUNA

Once they finally had the five million stem cells, the doctors froze them and made plans for the Big Kahuna—the mother of all chemo treatments—the one whose main objective was to wipe out my entire immune system. It would require another hospital stay with even harsher chemo than the superharsh chemo I gotten to kill the cancer. My old immune system apparently wasn't up to the task of searching out and killing off abnormal cancer cells. A brand new one would give me a better chance at sealing the remission deal and not having a recurrence.

I checked into the hospital at the end of January 2014 for the four days of BEAM chemo (another acronym of chemicals it turns out—nothing to do with beams of any kind) in preparation for the transplant. One day of "rest" and then they'd give me back my previously harvested stem cells. And this was when it went south for me. I had tolerated all five rounds of harsh chemo remarkably well. I had had very few side effects and mostly felt fatigue as a result. But when I went back to the Apheresis ward at SCCA to get the stem cells put back in, my body said, "WTF, Laren?!" I started vomiting. The nurse said I may be reacting to the preservative that they store the stem cells in. Since I had to have three harvesting sessions, I may be reacting to the amount of preservative. The doctors didn't want me to go home to recover, preferring to admit me back into the hospital, but I insisted. I was really sick of hospitals after the five hospital stays for the chemo treatments, and I desperately wanted to recover at home.

I was home for five days when the fever and diarrhea hit, both of which I have never experienced to this extreme in my entire life. I was checked into the hospital, dashing any dream I had of recovering at home. The doctors couldn't figure out what was causing the 104-degree fever and gave me stronger and stronger antibiotics until they finally decided to give me a broad spectrum one that would kill every little bacteria in my body—the good and the bad.

This was a huge bummer for me. As a health coach, I knew that even one round of antibiotics in a person's lifetime can wreak havoc on that delicate balance of good and bad bacteria in the gut. I knew what round after round of harsher and harsher antibiotics was doing to my system. So much for all that work I had done trying to balance my gut flora with seasonal whole foods detoxes.

The days of high fever and diarrhea were dark days filled with delusion and despair. The doctors wanted to help me somehow so kept offering me pain medicine even though I wasn't really in much pain. The pain meds (along with the fever) made me unable to distinguish reality from dream state as I drifted in and out. I became paranoid of the nursing staff and too wired to sleep deeply. To my doctors' disbelief, I chose to go off the pain meds entirely.

Through all of this, my mother slept in my hospital room, taking care of me as only a mother can. She had wiped my bum as a baby, and was again as my life hung on the brink. My husband, Ted, took care of the kids and came to the hospital every day, offering support but not knowing what to do. He relayed dire messages to my family (I found out later). Later when I was out of the woods and was no longer on IV fluids and could eat again, my friend Heidi, who hates hospitals by the way, brought me organic healthy food every day, a happy upbeat energy, and literally anything I needed or wanted. I was so grateful for everyone.

After five days of fever hell, it finally broke and reduced from 104 degrees to 101 degrees. It stayed there for a couple more days, but they didn't seem concerned about it. Eventually it went down to normal, and the diarrhea stopped. I was left with what they called "high-grade inflammation" in my entire GI tract. Great. But, hey, I was alive! I had made it through the worst hell I've ever been dealt. And I had thought having babies was hard!

Since the chemo had left me with no immune system, the hospital staff needed to keep close tabs on me. Any little germ that might be no big deal for an ordinary person could be very serious for me. The next step was crossing fingers and waiting to see if the brand new baby stem cells did what they were supposed to do and notice, "Hey where did the immune system go? We better rebuild that."

How the doctors could tell if the stem cells were doing their job was to monitor my blood. For some reason, this blood draw had to be done at midnight every night, making it very hard to get any rest. Believe me, I made requests to change this routine, but the hospital staff insisted it had to be at midnight. The doctors wouldn't let me leave the hospital until my neutrophils (the particular white blood cells that fight germs and bacteria) were above the golden number of six hundred. For me this took an excruciatingly long sixteen days.

This was an eternity, especially because the food was terrible, and, as I said, it's practically impossible to get any sleep in a hospital. By the time I was up to six hundred, I was climbing the walls and begging to be released.

It was during this waiting for the magic six hundred number that my hair fell out for the second time. I first noticed it as I was sitting in the hospital bed, and I pulled on it, and it came out in my hand in a big chunk. It was a good two inches long by then. I was bored and found this pulling of my hair fascinating since it didn't hurt. I pulled out chunks as I chatted with my mother, who watched me with horror/fascination. "That doesn't hurt, honey?" she asked. "Not at all." I got distracted by a nurse coming in to take my vitals, who surprisingly said nothing about my now patchy hair. I forgot about it until I decided to get up and wash my hands, seeing myself in the mirror. I was shocked to see my reflection. "How come you didn't tell me I looked like a clown?" I asked my mother. I had pulled out most of the top but left plenty around the sides and ears. I immediately put her on the task of making sure it was all out. I couldn't believe the nurse had not had the slightest reaction. I think that says a lot for nurses, really. They are angels on earth.

I was eventually sent home to do the rest of my recovery there. My mom needed to get back to my pre-Alzheimer's dad, whom my brothers had flown up to take care of so that Mom could tend to me. My mother-in-law Jacki flew up from Arizona and took care of me for the first couple of weeks at home. It was comforting to have her there, and she took good care of me, and I was grateful.

My recovery from the stem cell transplant took months. And months. I was so weak. I slept and slept, sleeping on average eleven hours a night. I was told to walk every day, and for the most part I did. My first walk was about a half a block down my road on my husband's arm. Then the next day I went a little farther. There was one day, a few weeks out, when I attempted a little half-mile loop with my husband, and I broke down halfway, crying by the side of the road, unsure if I could make it the rest of the way home. It took us forty-five minutes to walk half a mile. This from a woman who could walk/jog three to five miles with no problem just a year before.

11

HOW IT WAS FOR MY HUBBY

My husband, Ted, is very capable, and like most husbands, above all wants his wife to be happy. This experience was really hard on him. He was stoic and supportive and picked up the slack. He did everything that I used to do that wasn't being handled by one of our friends. He felt really uncomfortable accepting the generosity of our friends actually. He felt it reflected on him as a provider. "Do they think we don't have enough money for food for dinner? Stop telling your friends to bring casseroles." I told him over and over that they wanted to do something, and making a casserole was something they knew would help.

He was under an enormous amount of stress with his business and stress from my fragile health and not showing any of it to me because he felt I certainly didn't need to carry any of his burden. I am sure his family was checking in on him, but I suspect that he was telling them something along the lines of, "It's hard, but we're fine." As a result, I don't think his family and friends were as supportive of him as they would have wanted to have been had they known how much stress he was under.

Ted is generally an optimistic person. Tall, dark and handsome, goofy and lighthearted, he is kind and generous and was determined to support me in any way that he could. Not hindering my healing efforts by adding any of his burden to mine was an act of love. I knew he was stressed, but I also knew I needed to go within and focus on my healing and didn't have the bandwidth to help him much. He was right not to share his stress with me, although I do wish I could have helped.

As I said, my kids both started new schools at the same time that my chemo started, which meant that I couldn't help with that transition. I had to just hope for the best. This really went against my regular parenting style. I was a very involved parent and put my kids as a priority. However, right then, I was singularly focused on saving my own life.

Our daughter, who was starting seventh grade, studied hard, and (subconsciously?) deciding not to add stress to our already stressful situation, got straight As. Our son, who was starting high school, checked out, participated minimally, and barely passed his classes. I don't know if he was (subconsciously) trying to get my attention by doing poorly in school. Or maybe he had an "I don't give a crap; my mother might be dying" attitude. I just knew he was making very little effort. In the spring, when I had a bit more energy, I met with his teachers and asked them to consider the circumstances. He was allowed to do makeup work and made it through by the skin of his teeth.

All of this with the kids, plus trouble at his business with one of his business partners, was extremely stressful for Ted. He didn't talk too much about it. I appreciate the soldiering he did on my behalf, but I do wish he had let more people in.

I have heard people say that cancer is harder on the spouse than the patient. I'm not sure it's harder since they don't have to go through the physical destruction, but I get where they're coming from and would agree that it's at least as hard on the spouse as the patient. I appreciate all that Ted did for me throughout those two years. It was very hard on both of us.

12

THE CHALLENGE OF ACCEPTANCE

Along with all of the physical trials, I had emotional trials as well. I knew two people who had gone through stem cell transplants and had recovered at home, not getting a fever and not needing to go into the hospital at all. One even walked a mile every day posttransplant. Why wasn't I that strong? Why was my body having such a hard time with this? My identity of being a strong and healthy woman, as I had always been, was seriously put into question. To say that I was disappointed is a huge understatement. I had been doing everything right, and I got cancer. I really didn't know who I was on a fundamental level.

I'd see the promotions of my health coach colleagues with their fall and winter programs in place, and it was a bitter pill that this was not my path anymore. I knew that acceptance was the key here, but it was so challenging! I wanted to be promoting a fall detox! I want to be strong and healthy and networking and coaching clients to new levels of health and wellness! I wanted to be the healthy one, not the sick one.

One of the hardest parts of this whole diagnosis process was me losing my sense of self—the happy health coach, loving helping people get healthy. I was so sure of who I was, what I was doing, and where I was going, and had a plan to get there. Not only did all of those plans get turned on their heads, but who I was also flipped upside down.

In my late twenties, I went to a fortune teller in a corner shop in New York City just for the fun of it. She read my tarot cards and declared I would have a wonderful life. "No tragedies!" she'd said. I know some people will read this and think it's crazy or naïve, but I have clung to that prediction whenever I was in a scary situation, feeling confident that everything would turn out all right in the end because she had said, "No tragedies!" I believed that again now, all through this scary situation, trying to keep the faith of my fortune-teller destiny.

Acceptance. This has been a big word for me in this process. It came to me in a meditation after I had just had the diagnosis. "Pure acceptance," the Universe said to me, as the answer to the question, "What does my body need to heal?" (More on this experience in part 2.) At that point, I was looking for ways to reduce stress, and I heard that message to be about accepting the people in my life exactly as they are and to stop trying to change them. I listened and did some big work at that point and made some shifts for the better.

However, the questioning of my identity required a deeper level of acceptance. What we're talking about here was acceptance of this thing that was happening to me—this cancer that I was angry about and resentful of and wished beyond wished wasn't happening. How do you accept something like that? It has been a constant mental conversation for me and is one of the biggest lessons from this whole experience.

13

CANCER PART 2

Slowly, I recovered. It took a good nine months, but finally I started feeling like my old self again, physically as well as emotionally. I could walk the three-mile hilly route in my neighborhood without a problem. I was ready to get back in the game. I started focusing again on my business as a health coach and looking at what I wanted to do next. I enrolled in a business development course, and I got coaching from my business coach sister. I started using LinkedIn to promote a new career in corporate wellness. I met with people in HR at top companies in Seattle, pitching them on hiring me for Lunch and Learn Wellness Workshops and/or Corporate Health Coaching Programs. I was getting out there in the world. I wanted to incorporate my cancer experience, but I didn't want it to define me—it was part of my story now, but it was behind me. It was in my past—until it wasn't.

In December of 2014, I got a routine CT scan as part of my one-year posttransplant checkup. I had had these before, one at three months posttransplant, and one at six months. They had both been clear, and I was feeling so great; I was sure this one would be clear too. Well, the lymph nodes looked clear, but there was a little spot on the left breast that they wanted to look at more closely.

The left breast? Wasn't there something about the left breast way back from my very first MRI for the lymphoma? A spot they thought was maybe something, but they decided it must be a lymph node because the odds of having lymphoma and breast cancer at the same time are like lightning striking a person twice? Yes, that left breast. That same spot. There are lots of lymph nodes on the outside edge of the breast near this spot. It could be the lymphoma back again. And there was a remote chance it was breast cancer. I was scheduled quickly for a mammogram, and then walked directly across the hall for an ultrasound. When the nurse suggested an immediate biopsy, (there was that word again) I asked as my throat choked with fear, that my husband, who had been sitting all that time out in the waiting area, be brought in. They poked a needle in four spots for the biopsy, and afterward I could tell the technician knew it was cancer by the way she was talking to me. She actually said, "I know this is the worst news you could get." I'm thinking, *Didn't you just say the results would take a few days?* She knew the results weren't going to be good.

The worst part of getting a biopsy is the waiting. I prepared myself for the worst—that the mantle cell was back. That would mean an attempt at another stem cell transplant, this time from a donor, or maybe some experimental new drug. The other possibility was breast cancer, but that was just so unlikely. My doctor called me on January 2. He said, "The good news is that there was no sign of mantle cell in the biopsy. The bad news is that it is breast cancer. And the important part is that it is triple negative breast cancer—the more rare and aggressive variety." Why do I always get the more rare and aggressive varieties?

Here we go again. Shock. Disbelief. Once again that knowing that I had done everything right, and it didn't turn out. I had taken all of the herbs and supplements religiously. And speaking of religion, I had even incorporated my version of the spiritual side. I had been meditating, and opening up to spirituality. And, of course, I was still eating superhealthfully. This lesson of acceptance was once again upon me. Shit happens. Accept it.

Cancer is so strange. It's such a big bad disease, and yet you don't feel a thing initially. Once again, I felt great. I hadn't even felt the lump. Normally, our bodies give us clues when we are sick. We have a stuffy nose, or we feel tired, or we have a pain in our side. Cancer isn't like that. It's a silent killer. It sneaks up on you when you're least expecting it. This second diagnosis really sealed the feeling that I could no longer trust my body. I wasn't in tune. Maybe it's not possible to tune in. This is something I had coached my clients to do—to dial into the language of their bodies, to listen to the clues their bodies are giving them. I didn't have a clue. Once again I was left unsure and feeling vulnerable when I was so used to feeling strong and healthy. I had been just starting to feel like I was back to my old self, back in the game, but apparently *not*. This not knowing, this uncertainty of the health of my body, continues to be one of the hardest parts of having these cancer diagnoses.

14

ACCEPTANCE. AGAIN

So here I was with another "opportunity" for acceptance. I had more tough choices and more doctor appointments and was on the roller coaster once again. Really, this was just so sad. It was really too much to believe. I had already been through so much. Why did I have to go through more? I asked my doctor if the breast cancer was what they call a secondary cancer from the mantle cell. This is when you get cancer from the treatment itself or from the increased susceptibility to cancer after treatment. He said he didn't think so. The secondary cancers come years later. What was more likely is that I had both of these cancers at the same time, and the breast cancer got knocked back by the hyper-CVAD but not wiped out. With my low immune system from the stem cell transplant, it got an opportunity to rebuild. It didn't show up on the three-month and six-month scans because it was still undetectable at that point.

I wallowed in the despair of my fate for a good three days. Two cancers at once? I cried and cried. My family didn't know what to do with me. I stayed in my room. I could not stop crying. Finally, maybe wrung dry of tears, I picked myself up. It occurred to me that I had already been through the absolute worst. I had already had the worst chemo they give anybody and had survived. How bad could this be? They had caught it early; the tumors were relatively small. They could even cut them out—which hadn't been an option with the blood cancer.

So I rallied. I interviewed friends who had been through breast cancer. Unfortunately, I discovered I knew quite a few. Some had single mastectomies, some had double. Some had reconstruction, and some of them hadn't. I went to work selecting my team and making appointments. I had been through this before. I had some experience this time around. I set to interviewing the doctors, to see with whom I wanted to work. Before, I had felt lucky to get my excellent lymphoma doctor. But there were a lot of good breast cancer oncologists in Seattle. I wanted the best. I took a power position and considered myself hiring them for the job. It was a completely different attitude, and I liked it.

I decided on a double mastectomy with skin and nipple sparing for reconstruction. Both sides just to be on the safe side for recurrence and, to be honest, so that I was balanced for the new boobage. Also, they had seen some abnormal cells on the other breast that were not yet cancerous, a watch and wait situation, and I just didn't want to worry about it. A mastectomy had been recommended because of the location of the tumors and because there appeared to be three of them. They would have had to take so much of the tissue once they got the margins that I wouldn't be left with much of a breast anyway.

I chose my top-notch surgeon, met with him, and scheduled the surgery. My surgeon did an amazing job. (At least every doctor and nurse who checked out his work told me they looked "gorgeous."

"Gorgeous," I figured, was relative, considering I had Shar-Pei dog style extra skin, flat as a pancake breasts, and three-inch scars from nipple to each armpit. But I'll take "gorgeous" when given). Thankfully, I got through the postop drain situation fairly easily. This was an icky bit of pumping and measuring fluids that I had never experienced before, never having had any kind of major surgery. My sister-in-law Pat came up and took care of me postop. She was *the best* nurse. She is by nature one of the kindest, mellowest, most loving people I know. She is also a fabulous french-style chef, making delicious and nutritious meals for us. We were sad to see her go after five days, and wished she could have just moved in. The offer stands!

Even after Pat left, all went well, and I got to have the drains removed at ten days on the left side and fourteen days on the right. I was declared barely in the stage 2 category because one of the tumors was 6 cm and anything 5-10 cm puts you in stage 2. There was no lymph node involvement, which was a really good thing. However, because it was triple negative, meaning none of the three receptors usually on breast cancer cells were estrogen receptive, I would be getting chemo again.

This brought up the same natural remedies question from before. Could I do this with alternative therapies? Could I not get chemo? I asked the naturopathic oncologist and the regular oncologist. Both said that triple negative is a different kind of beast. It was just too aggressive. Those other therapies, while helpful, wouldn't be strong enough to effectively get rid of any random cancer cells floating around in my bloodstream. There would be a higher likelihood of recurrence. This was the type of breast cancer people died from. I continue to get criticism and judgment from the health and alternative crowd on the Internet, who don't believe in chemotherapy. All I can say is I hope they never have to make this choice because it is a tough one. Every cancer is unique, and you have to decide on an individual basis. I will never judge people for the treatment that they choose.

15

SHOPPING FOR BOOBS

I decided to get prosthetic breasts to wear until the reconstruction, which couldn't start until two months after the chemo was complete. I made an appointment at the lingerie department at Nordstrom and asked my friend Jana if she'd come with me. I was a bit nervous and thought it best to have a girlfriend for moral support. Nordstrom offers this service for free for mastectomy patients (Isn't that amazing of them? I love Nordstrom). They have a variety of silicone breasts in different sizes there to try on and see how they look. I hadn't shown my boobless chest with its two three-inch horizontal scars from nipple to armpit to anyone but my husband and my doctor at that point. I asked the young salesgirl if she was ready before I took off my shirt. She said she'd seen it all before and was so kind and reassuring. She brought different size prosthetics and a variety of bras to try on.

My girlfriend Jana was a big help in lightening the mood and making it fun. I encouraged her to get measured, and it turned out she was my old size, so bonus! She got five barely worn bras from me as hand-me-downs.

I ended up going a couple cup sizes smaller than I was before. I chose super comfortable rather practical-looking bras, one in nude and one in black. But I highly recommend getting something lacy or racy if you think it might lift your spirits to wear it. We can all use a little boost, especially mastectomy patients! The prosthetics and the bras were all covered on my insurance. Nordstrom will sew the flaps that hold the prosthetics in place into any bra you choose free of charge. I wore them when I felt like it, but I often went flat-chested.

Surprisingly, I have been fairly neutral emotionally about losing my breasts. I had a lot more of my identity tied up with my hair, as it turns out, than I did with my breasts. In a way I was relieved that they could remove the cancer in this way, unlike with the lymphoma. I liked my DD cup breasts, but large breasts also take management (you large-breasted women know what I'm talking about) so, in the vein of looking for the positives in all of this, going a couple of cup sizes smaller was a good thing.

I have friends, though, for whom cutting off this part of their anatomy was a very emotional experience. Everyone's journey is different, and every emotion is valid. One friend told me that going through reconstruction was very emotional, and every expansion brought up anew the sadness of getting cancer. What's important as a friend is to be supportive; let each individual feel what they're feeling and have it be completely okay however they're going through it. Because it's okay to feel however you feel, and at the same time so totally not okay that you got cancer at all.

Reconstruction consisted of another surgery where they first put in "expanders" under my pectoral muscles but using the same incision they cut for the mastectomy. Again, I had to be knocked out, but it wasn't full anesthesia this time, just enough to snooze during the procedure. I was nervous but not as much as before. I must be getting used to surgeries!

The plastic surgeon inserted and then partially filled little crescent-shaped pieces of plastic with fluid. He then added saline fluid over the next weeks to expand the pectoral muscles gradually, creating scar tissue, which is actually what eventually holds the implant in place. This process wasn't particularly painful for me, more like a pressure feeling. Once the perfect size for my frame was achieved, the implants were swapped out for the expanders. I must say it's nice to not have to wear a bra anymore. Gotta' keep looking for the positives!

16

CHEMO. AGAIN.

Before the reconstruction could begin, though, I had to again have chemo to kill any random breast cancer cells that might be floating around in my body. Even though my lymph nodes were clear, they did find some in the lymph pathway, indicating that the tumors had started splitting off cells to invade other parts of the body. The difference between this cancer and the lymphoma was that there was no way to detect the random cells. With lymphoma, it was in my blood, so they could take a sample and declare "remission." With triple negative breast cancer, there's no way to know how many, if any, random cells are floating around, and then no way to test if the chemo actually got them. Some holistic health coaches at this point would have said, "No, thank you. No more chemo for me. Let's try a more holistic natural approach this time." Or maybe they'd just watch and wait and hope their healthy living would keep the cancer at bay. I didn't have that sense of security anymore.

Having been rocked by the lymphoma diagnosis and my healthy lifestyle letting me down, I didn't have faith that it alone would work. I wanted to do what would give me the highest chance of meeting my grandchildren. I took my oncologist's advice and went for the preventative chemo.

And again, the acceptance lesson reared its lovely head. "Why me?" was a constant refrain in my head. When my new highly recommended breast cancer oncologist explained the chemo protocol, it all sounded familiar and way easier than what I'd already been through. I felt like I could do this.

Just as I suspected, the first phase of breast cancer chemo, Taxol, wasn't anything like the hyper-CVAD. It was only an hour a week, and once again I tolerated it well. My oncologist was concerned about my bone marrow having gone through the wringer the year before with the transplant and rightly so because after only two treatments of Taxol, the gentler of the three chemos in my treatment plan, my bone marrow said, "Forget this!" A blood test showed that my neutrophils were back down to an all-time low since the transplant, a mere three hundred (remember how they wouldn't let me leave the hospital until I was at six hundred?). It was disconcerting considering it had taken me a good six months to get my neutrophil count just into the normal range of above one thousand. And now with only two little one-hour chemo treatments, it was back down to nil.

Luckily, they have drugs for this situation. It wasn't too long ago that a patient would have had to wait until her neutrophil numbers were up to get another round of chemo. But now they have Neupogen, a drug made from human growth cells, the ones that tell the bone marrow to start making white blood cells. I got a shot that day and was sent home with three more to give myself each evening in my belly. The needle was super skinny, and I had some experience with this before with the lymphoma when they thought I had a blood clot, and I had to give myself shots for that. Not too bad once I got used to it. Phase 1 for me was twelve weekly doses of Taxol. By mid-June, I was finished with it and celebrating a minimilestone.

The second phase of chemo, a combo of Adramycin and Cytoxin (AC), was a little harsher than the first, which for me meant that I was a bit more fatigued than with the Taxol, which I didn't notice too much. I had had both of these drugs with my hyper-CVAD chemo, so that unknown factor was diminished, and I felt confident I could handle these. My bone marrow, however, gave up fully and needed an even bigger booster shot with the AC, so we switched Neupogen shots to Neulasta, a stronger and longer-lasting version, which I got shots of at the time of treatment. In what they call the nadir, the low point between treatments, which were two weeks apart now, my neutrophils actually got all the way to zero at one point. That was a first since the stem cell transplant! More antibiotics were needed when I got a mild fever. Again with the antibiotics! I would have a lot of gut health work to do after this was all over. There were only three of these treatments every two weeks, and finally, *finally*, after six long months, I was done with it.

Every week during those six months, my best friend, Heidi, and/or other friends kept me company. We met beforehand at a close by juice bar, and I got a Green Juice to set my body up for the upcoming onslaught of nasty "medicine." Having that love and support from my friends each week was so special and touching. Their company, conversation, and funny stories all made the time fly by. I really have the best girlfriends.

I celebrated my last chemo treatment on August 5 with several besties, one of whom, Colleen, snuck a bottle of champagne into the chemo ward. With plastic champagne flutes, we popped the bubbly and toasted the end to my chemotherapy. It was a great day.

Part 2

HOW I GOT THROUGH THE DIAGNOSIS AND TREATMENT WITH STRENGTH AND OPTIMISM

I went through a lot with my two back-to-back cancer diagnoses and treatments, and I also learned a lot. That's what this section is for. Memoirs are great and valuable, but I wanted to expand on the lessons I learned, some of them pretty profound for me. I also wanted to give some how-to-style advice for the cancer patient who has just been diagnosed and is in the soup of the fear and turmoil. I've been there and believe this section can help.

In this part 2, I've assembled my thoughts and lessons into seven sections. I've also included an Appendix of Tips for the Cancer Patient, Things They Don't Tell You about Chemo, and What Not to Say to a Cancer Patient. All of these things I learned the hard way.

My hope is to empower you, the newly diagnosed cancer patient, to take this disease on and kick its ass. Hit it from every angle: starve it to death by not feeding it what it likes, wash it in healing energy through visualizations, get into your body's healing space through meditation, attack it with optimism and positivity, get support from loved ones, and find peace through gratitude and acceptance.

May you find strength in your work against this disease, and may you find love, peace, and gratitude for your life on this big blue ball in space, however it's been and however it turns out.

"I learned that courage was not the absence of fear, but the triumph over it. The brave man is not he who does not feel afraid, but he who conquers that fear."—Nelson Mandela

1

FIND YOUR INNER WARRIOR.

Getting a cancer diagnosis is by far the scariest thing that has ever happened to me. My mind started spinning with all of the "what ifs." What if I die and don't get to see my kids grow up? What if I don't get to meet my grandchildren? What if it's painful? What if, what if, what if. It is all so scary that I can completely understand how some people shut down, cannot function, and basically want to curl up in a ball and cry for days. That is all good for a time, a short time really, because what is needed is for you to dig down and find your inner warrior. You need to gather your courage and strength, your warrior strength, and fight for the future you want to have.

When my brother Jeff was first diagnosed, I called him, and we talked about this idea. He was certain from what the doctors said that he had only a short time to live. He was resigned to this fact. And it was true that his situation was dire. The lung cancer had metastasized to his brain and bones. But I said the same thing to him. You need to find your inner warrior. Fight this fight. Do the most you can to live as long as you can. He was fighting for his son and wife and for the future he wanted with them. It helped to give him hope and the possibility of a different outcome.

A week later, when I came down to visit, he told me stories of using the inner warrior to block negativity from doctors and well-meaning friends who say unintentionally insensitive things, such as the research they've done on what his odds were of surviving the disease (or not!). He shared with me that in those cases, he put up his warrior shield and blocked the negative thoughts. He replied, "Hmmm, well, that won't be me." He did live longer than anyone expected, and for a time seemed to have shrunk the cancer tumors in his body to nearly nothing, including somehow the tumors in his brain even though the chemo wasn't supposed to be able to cross the blood-brain barrier. In the end, the cancer was too strong. He died before any of us were ready for him to go—way too young, way too much still yet to contribute to his family, his wife and young son, and the world.

In my journey, the inner warrior needed to come out with the mere mention of the words biopsy and oncologist—scary words you never want to hear from your doctor. I steeled myself for more scary words throughout all of those preliminary doctor appointments where they were trying to figure out what was wrong. I immediately shoved the possibility that I would die way back in Denial Land and shut the door. After that point, I only focused on doing what I had to do to move forward with survival. Strangely, death barely entered my mind again.

I mentioned in part 1 that I'm not sure if this was smart or not, but when I told my kids that I had been diagnosed with a rare form of non-Hodgkins lymphoma, and that I was going to be getting chemo for it, and life would be a bit different for a while, I actually told them that I wasn't going to die. I was so resolute that this wasn't a possibility that I felt okay in saying that to them. I feel strongly that determination and a strong mental state factor in to the strength with which you are willing to fight.

What I focused on was all that I would miss if cancer won and how that was just not acceptable. For me, the primary focus was seeing my kids grow up. The idea of this not happening was just not allowed. I would see my kids grow up, get married, and have children of their own. I would live to be a grandmother, and I was now going to fight to make sure of it. That continues to be the goal.

Even so, at some point I (stupidly) went online to see what the statistics were for mantle cell. I got this feeling at a doctor's appointment that people knew something dire that they weren't telling me. I went to a non-Hodgkins lymphoma website and clicked on the mantle cell button. I then saw a "Prognosis" button and clicked. As I read, I became more and more stunned. I found out that I had a 5 percent chance of living five years. How did I not know this?! I then realized that my doctors had never told me my prognosis. My main doctor is world-renowned and is the best in his field, and I have immense confidence in him. He has only ever been positive in his attitude, and it was infectious. He was incredibly certain that we would get to remission.

But unfortunately, once you learn something, you can't unlearn it. I now knew the scary facts and inadvertently opened the door to fear. Fear is a real ally to cancer and has no place in the cancer fight. Fear and worry do nothing helpful. They undermine the positive mental attitude that is so vitally important for healing to occur. When I first read the statistics, I cried and suddenly was very scared. I confessed to my husband that I had looked up my prognosis. As I suspected, he had already done that research and knew the results. He comforted me and reminded me that I would get through it.

At my next appointment, I didn't mention to my doctor that I knew the prognosis. I understood and appreciated why he had never told me this information. It wasn't statistically relevant to me. The people in those studies weren't me, and I was young and strong and could handle this. He had faith in my abilities, and so I did too.

Besides, I'm not the type of person that has ever wallowed for long in despair. I knew fear wouldn't help me heal. To get myself out of the fear-based mind-set, I developed a practice of checking in with myself whenever I felt fear. I would ask myself, "How am I right now?" Invariably, I found that right this minute, I was fine. This practice of Being Here Now actually had me feel grateful to be alive and strong, and I found that I was able to keep optimistic.

I used this trick frequently during my months of treatment. I found that with each new chemo drug (and I got eight of them between the two cancers) I was afraid of what might happen and of how my body might react. For the mantle cell, I was getting the harshest chemo they give anybody. I was afraid it might be really bad. I imagined things from movies like having convulsions, or foaming at the mouth. I really had no idea what I was getting myself into. During these thought spirals, I began the habit of checking in with my body and found that right now, I was fine. And thankfully, I tolerated them all well.

The Nonviolent Warrior

In the cancer world, there is a lot of language and energy around being a fighter, imagining your white blood cells in battle, killing the cancer cells. But I am not a violent person. I'm the type that catches bees and spiders that have lost their way into our house, releasing them outside. And even though I knew that it was either cancer or me, and I had to win, I wanted a way to do it nonviolently.

I got great suggestions from friends, and in the end chose a practice suggested by my good friend and acupuncturist Erin. She had fought a similar battle with her mother and was in tune with vibrations and energies through her practice. After one of my acupuncture treatments, we were talking in her hallway. I told her how I didn't want to be violent; I just wanted the cancer to go away. She suggested a great idea. She said, "In your daily meditations, you could visualize a healing white light pouring in through the top of your head, bathing your cells in healing energy." I loved the sound of this. There were a few places that I knew cancer was hanging out from the PT/CT scans. So while I meditated, I visualized those enlarged lymph nodes getting smaller and the white light shrinking the cancer cells. I also started speaking to the cancer. I told it that it was not welcome in this body and that it needed to go. I watched as the healing white light traveled to all of my bones, washing the bone marrow and shrinking any cell that was abnormal.

Another friend suggested that I name the cancer, preferably a name starting with *N* (I'm not sure why—n for negative rather than positive?). I assumed that naming the cancer is a way to separate it from yourself and give it its own identity apart from yours. In doing so, I assumed that it would be easier to talk to and encourage it to shrivel up and die. I played around with several names that began with *N*. My first thought was Nancy. Fancy Nancy not welcome here. Or Norma Jean, like "Goodbye, Norma Jean …" In the end I chose Norm, short for Abby Normal, the name of the brain given to the monster in *Young Frankenstein*. This made me laugh as I thought it might be the name of someone I'd rather not hang out with. From then on, I spoke directly to Norm during my daily visualizations and told him that the party was over, and he wasn't welcome in my body. Ever again. Time to say good-bye. Sayonara, baby.

I did this every day for at least a half hour each time. It was empowering, and I felt like I was able to take control of part of my healing when my life felt so totally out of my control. I also felt calm, centered, and peaceful as a result of the daily meditation (more on meditation later).

After remission, it's important that the inner warrior remain focused and keep working to maintain remission because it's easy to slip back into old unhealthy habits. For me, my inner warrior has been working hard to keep my life in balance—staying optimistic, exercising daily, remaining calm, and quieting my inner perfectionist. This is a challenge actually, and I've noticed a tendency to slip back into old patterns of not doing the self-care rituals that were so important during my treatment. My type A personality likes to be productive and tends to choose productivity over self-care. My inner warrior does fiercely defend my need for a low-stress, mellow home life with my teenagers, and demands time to keep a balanced life. It is so tempting to go back to what was normal. But I know I must maintain a new cancer-free normal.

This kind of self-care is important for everyone, not just cancer patients. It's challenging in our hectic, stressful, fast-paced society to stay calm and centered, present to the miracles of each day. I assert that having a practice of meditation as well as other self-care practices such as being in nature and laughing a lot would greatly improve our planet as well as the people on it.

I can hear my mom friends saying, "Sounds great, but who has the time?" A few key behaviors are required here: making your self-care a top priority, planning it into your day, and asking for help if needed. I have friends who do this, and I noticed that my husband does it. I realized I needed to stop asking if taking some time for myself works for his schedule. What if I assumed that my self-care was absolutely a priority, and I just needed to inform him of when it would be happening? Kind of like how he does with me. And I know there are children to feed and all that. We type-A, perfectionist, I-can-do-it-all types don't like to give up control. But burnout is right around the corner, baby. And with burnout comes exhaustion, with a little resentment thrown in, which can lead to disease. Asking for help from friends, neighbors, *husbands*, is the key to successful self-care.

Postremission, it's also important to maintain healthy eating. In the next chapter I go into how food is definitely a factor in your health, everyone's health—not just cancer patients. I think that it's because I was eating so healthfully before getting cancer that I was able to get through the harsh treatments as well as I did. It's in everyone's best interest to be as healthy as possible in order to be otherwise strong in case illness hits. So I maintain a healthy, clean diet, even having improved on it some posttreatment. I'm not taking any chances.

"All disease begins in the gut."—Hippocrates

2

FOCUS ON THE PHYSICAL

Clean Up Your Diet and Go Organic

I have been a board certified health and nutrition coach for six years now, having coached over one hundred clients, individually and in groups, to achieve their goals. The most common goal was weight loss, but there were also people who wanted to quit sugar, had digestive issues, low energy, joint pain, were prediabetic, or had Hashimoto's (thyroid) disease. Looking at what they were eating, figuring out what their unique bodies liked and didn't like, made a difference for every single one of them. In the United States, we are a melting pot of all different ethnicities, and they bring all their different delicious cuisines with them. But genetically, our digestive systems are not set up to eat every kind of food on the planet. For example, someone of Japanese heritage genetically has a digestive system wired to easily digest a lot of fish and rice. Give these people hamburgers and a big glass of milk, and their bodies scream foul. Their immune systems think it is poison, and it causes chronic low-grade inflammation over time. This is what the research is showing is the precursor to all of the big bad diseases[5]: cancer, heart disease, Alzheimer's, diabetes, and arthritis, to name a few. It is critical that we each figure out what kinds of foods our unique bodies like and don't like for long-term health and wellness.

Having said all that, there are certain foods that no human body thrives on. Processed foods—as in anything white: white flour, white rice, white sugar, and non-whole-grain cereals—are one such category. These foods create an inflammatory environment in your body, and guess what thrives in an inflamed environment? Cancer![6] So if you've been thinking you should clean up your diet, as a cancer patient, or even as someone who doesn't want to get cancer, now would be a great time. I highly recommend an anti-inflammatory diet for everyone.

Know that old saying "You are what you eat?" Well, it is literally true. The food you eat breaks down and fuels your cells, and how nutrient dense that food is is directly proportional to how vital and strong your cells are. Since your body is made up of these cells, building your health from a cellular level is a good idea. There's another old saying, "Eat your vegetables." That one's also true. Diets that are mostly plants have been shown to be better for cancer prevention, as well as other chronic disease.[7]

And, please, if you can, buy organic. The chemicals that are sprayed on vegetables, especially glyphosate, which has been declared by the World Health Organization to "probably cause cancer,"[8] are all nasty and not fit for human consumption. Why would you add cancer-causing chemicals to your diet when trying to heal from cancer?

I highly recommend checking out the Environmental Working Group's website, www.ewg.org; download their guide to the Dirty Dozen and the Clean Fifteen. These are guidelines for what are the most and least pesticide-sprayed fruits and vegetables.

I will go more into each of these, but here are five pretty basic rules to live by that will help fight cancer and build your strength for the fight as well as help in cancer prevention:

- Make half your plate vegetables (preferably organic) at every meal.
- Reduce or, better yet, eliminate sugar.
- Drink lots of filtered water.
- Reduce refined foods.
- Eat small portions of high-quality proteins.

Following these simple rules set me up to be in a really healthy and strong position from which to fight the cancer that was trying to take over my body. I really think the fact that I was otherwise in really good shape was a key factor in how well I did with my treatment. It's important to be physically strong to fight the onslaught of the chemotherapy if needed.

Eating this way will set your body up to be a healthy environment and thus a less hospitable host for those nasty cancer cells. It will also make you strong for the battle ahead. For people who want to take it up a notch, I recommend a few more rules: eat plenty of good fats, eliminate alcohol and caffeine, stop eating anything fried, and research an anti-inflammatory diet for all of its health benefits. But let's begin with the basics.

If you've been diagnosed with cancer, your immune system has failed you on some level because it is supposed to be on the lookout for abnormal cells growing out of control. But it may not necessarily have been your immune system's fault. Cancer is sneaky and can cloak itself to be undetectable by the immune system. There are a million random ways that cancer cells form, from environmental toxins to pesticides, to genetic abnormalities. But one of the things I learned while rebuilding my immune system from literally nothing, is that there are T cells in your immune system whose job it is to track down and kill off abnormal cells. For whatever reason, my immune system didn't or couldn't track down and kill the abnormal cells that grew out of control and into mantle cell lymphoma and breast cancer.

It makes sense to boost those T cells, helping your immune system do its job to heal and kill off the cancer cells. Some exciting research is being done in this kind of immunotherapy to fight cancer.[9] The researchers are learning how to help our immune systems seek out particular markers on cancer cells, even the ones that have figured out how to cloak themselves or otherwise hide from our killer T cells. Great news! Go science!

Vegetables

Feed your body a wide variety of colorful (particularly dark green like kale, broccoli, and cabbage) cancer-fighting vegetables, and cut out anything that is going to compromise those T cells' ability to find and destroy the abnormal cancer cells. A great cookbook I used while I was in treatment was *The Cancer-Fighting Kitchen*, by Rebecca Katz. Supplements are also good, and I took a lot under the supervision of my naturopathic oncologist. Among others she prescribed, based on the particular phase I was in my treatment, I regularly took omega-3 fish oil capsules, extra vitamin C, green tea extract, turmeric, and vitamin D3. I read recently in *Scientific American* that in order for our T cells to turn into cancer killers, there must be ample vitamin D.[10] So get fifteen minutes of sunshine every day and/or take a vitamin D3 supplement. I take 5,000 UI per day.

Also, mushrooms have been shown to kill cancer and boost your immune system, according to the National Institutes of Health.[11] All varieties have cancer-fighting properties, but my naturopathic oncologist recommended a few unusual varieties in particular: turkey tail, reishi, and cordyceps. You can get these online or at natural food stores. I recommend a brand called Host Defense Organic Mushrooms, out of Olympia, Washington. See your naturopathic doctor for dosing amounts or follow suggestions on the bottle.

Sugar

Sugar is one of the most inflammatory foods that you can eat.[12] As I mentioned earlier, cancer thrives in an inflammatory environment. Cutting back on sugar is not only going to create a less hospitable environment for cancer, it will also help reduce excess weight; help reduce inflammation in your arteries (particularly good for heart patients); help reduce inflammation in your brain for better cognitive function, which can be a possible side effect of some chemotherapies, and is good for people with Alzheimer's in their families; and help with mood swings. And who doesn't need help with mood swings when you're dealing with a cancer diagnosis? Sugar is highly addictive and is probably the number one worst thing you could be eating for a number of health reasons. Best to cut it out now that you have a serious diagnosis on your hands.

By the way, please do not switch to artificial sweeteners—they are worse! Studies show they actually cause weight gain instead of the opposite.[13] Besides, they are chemical concoctions, some of which have been shown to cause cancer in lab rats.[14] That's enough for me to not want them in my body. I suggest switching to whole fruit when you need something sweet. Switch to dark chocolate when you need a fix. Use a bit of natural sweetener, such as raw honey, real maple syrup, or stevia, to sweeten something a little. Your taste buds will eventually adjust. Your cravings will subside in just a few days.

Water

Americans are chronically dehydrated. We may drink coffee all day, but many people only get a few glasses of water in. Most medical professionals recommend we drink half our body weight in fluid ounces of good quality filtered water each day. Noncaffeinated drinks count toward that total. But if you're drinking coffee or tea all day, you actually need to drink extra water to compensate for the dehydrating qualities of the caffeine in those drinks. However, there actually can be too much of a good thing here, since drinking too much water (athletes are particularly susceptible) can be a problem. It's called hypernatremia, "in which the kidneys become overwhelmed by the large quantity of liquid it's forced to process. The body's naturally occurring sodium can't keep up with the amount of water, leading to swelling in the cells and in severe cases, death," according to *Medical Daily*.[15]

So as long as you don't overdo it, a few of the many benefits of being well hydrated are:

- Increases energy and relieves fatigue
- Flushes out toxins
- Improves skin complexion
- Maintains regularity
- Boosts immune system
- Natural headache remedy
- Boosts good mood

Clean Eating and Seasonal Detoxes

Eating "clean" and seasonal detoxes are having a moment in the health circles, and with good reason. Clean eating means eating food with no pesticides, from whole ingredients, wild or locally sourced meats without antibiotics, and avoiding known allergens. The most common foods people are allergic to include wheat, milk, soy, corn, and nuts. If you're going to be a true clean eater, though, you'll also avoid refined sugar, caffeine, and alcohol. The end result when you eat this way is that you feel fantastic—my seven-day detox clients have reported more energy, no more "brain fog," and better sleep at night, not to mention weight loss and reduced bloating. Imagine if you suddenly felt sharp and alert (without coffee!), your jeans fit every day, you no longer needed a nap at three in the afternoon, and you slept like a baby at night. When you're eating "clean," you are eating what your body likes rather than hard-to-digest foods. Your body is able to get back in balance and do some healing work. Your immune system isn't fighting foods to which it may be allergic or intolerant. My clients have naturally shed weight and have found it easy to maintain a healthy body.

If eating this way seems too hard or restrictive, I recommend taking steps in that direction as much as you can by making small adjustments. Find out if you're intolerant to a food and avoid just that one for a while, and see how you feel. Sometimes, people just cut out dairy (like I did five years ago) and find that there were symptoms they were living with that they had no idea were connected to the food they were eating. And unfortunately, when you are eating an offending food on a daily basis, your immune system is chronically fighting that perceived poison and is therefore possibly not scoping out those abnormal cancer cells to destroy. You want to be doing as much as you can to make your immune system stronger, not eating something that is straining it every day.

Seasonal Detoxes

Seasonal detoxes are a great way to reset your body and give it the opportunity to heal. A wide variety of these are on the market, and I recommend a whole foods approach. I'm not keen on advising my clients to drink their meals unless they're in a hurry and need to make a smoothie before they dash out the door. I feel that meals should be cooked and enjoyed sitting down, preferably with loved ones and over conversation and laughter. So the seasonal detoxes I do with my clients consist of whole foods, mostly soups and salads, eating clean as described above, for seven or fourteen days. Once you've given your body a bit of a rest from foods it may not like and have created a clean slate of sorts, it's a great opportunity to reintroduce the common allergens one at a time to see how your body reacts. You can learn what your unique body likes and doesn't like, and that's valuable information if you want to keep your immune system strong. I recommend doing either a weeklong, eleven-day, or fourteen-day whole foods clean eating reset with each new season.

The Human Microbiome

A tremendous amount of research is going into the legion of bacteria in and on our bodies, what the scientists call the human microbiome. What they've discovered is fascinating. In terms of this book for the cancer patient, it is important to note that there is experimental evidence associating the human microbiome, diet, and cancer.[16]

Here are some interesting facts about these little bugs:[17]

- Between 70 and 90 percent of the cells in and on our bodies are microbes, including bacteria.
- There are ten times more bacterial cells on your body than human cells.

- More than eight hundred types of bacteria live in the human gut—some are beneficial, and some are harmful.
- Our microbiome is continually influenced by environment, diet, and drugs.
- 80 percent of your immune system is in your gut.
- Just one dose of antibiotics upsets the balance.

I don't know what came first with me, my food intolerance or my gut imbalance. When I went in for a routine checkup with a naturopath five years ago, I discovered that I was allergic to dairy products. I had been eating cheese, yogurt, milk, and ice cream my whole life. How could I possibly be allergic to dairy? Well, my blood test indicated that I was, and what I have since found out is that my undiagnosed dairy intolerance could have caused an imbalance in gut bacteria, causing strain on my immune system.[18]

But it also can happen the other way around. I have also learned that a gut imbalance can cause food intolerances.[19] It looks like my dairy allergy was probably hereditary. I was probably born with it, since I've had minor symptoms my whole life, but never associated the symptoms with a food intolerance. But could the gut imbalance have come first? Possibly. It's definitely a chicken or egg situation.

Leaky Gut

Eating a poor diet, taking antibiotics, being under chronic stress, or being exposed to too many toxins can create a condition called leaky gut. With leaky gut, the poor diet, antibiotics, stress, and toxins damage cells in your intestines, which then don't produce the enzymes needed for proper digestion. As a result, your body can't absorb essential nutrients, which can lead to a weakened immune system as well as hormone imbalances.[20]

According to Dr. Leo Galland, director of the Foundation for Integrated Medicine, the following symptoms might be signs of leaky gut:[21]

- Chronic diarrhea, constipation, gas, or bloating
- Nutritional deficiencies
- Poor immune system
- Headaches, brain fog, memory loss
- Excessive fatigue
- Skin rashes and problems such as acne, eczema, or rosacea
- Cravings for sugar or carbs
- Arthritis or joint pain
- Depression, anxiety, ADD, ADHD
- Autoimmune diseases such as rheumatoid arthritis, lupus, celiac disease, or Crohn's

It's called leaky gut because what has happened is that small holes have been created in the lining of your gut, allowing through things that are supposed to stay inside your gut. Things such as gluten, bad bacteria, and even undigested food particles can get into your bloodstream. Toxic waste also can leak into your bloodstream, causing an immune reaction.

I have had antibiotics several times in my life. More recently, after the stem cell transplant, I had four rounds of superharsh antibiotics to get my fever down. Antibiotics are the most commonly prescribed medicine there is. Often prescribed unnecessarily, antibiotics kill *all* of the bacteria in the gut, the good and the bad, definitely upsetting the balance. With up to 80 percent of your immune system in your gut,[22] it's important to keep these bacteria happy!

Eating foods with naturally occurring probiotics, such as fermented foods (sauerkraut, yogurt, kimchi, and tempeh), helps reestablish some of the good bacteria that may have gotten killed off.[23] Also, a high-quality probiotic supplement may help. Consult your naturopathic doctor for a good brand and appropriate dose.

If left unrepaired, a gut imbalance can lead to more severe health issues such as inflammatory bowel disease, IBS, arthritis, muscle pain, and chronic fatigue. It can also lead to skin issues such as eczema and psoriasis, as well as brain issues such as depression, anxiety, and migraine headaches. It causes strain on your immune system, which can lead to chronic low-level inflammation. This is the kind of inflammation in our bodies that research is showing is the precursor to diabetes, heart disease, and, yes, even cancer.

Exercise

Of course, there is a ton of evidence for the many health benefits of exercising and avoiding a sedentary lifestyle. Staying active, such as walking, during your cancer treatment is one of the most important things you can do. Studies show that regular exercise boosts the effectiveness of chemotherapy.[24] Another interesting benefit for everyone, and cancer patients in particular, is that exercise also boosts your immune system,[25] which, as I mentioned earlier, is what cancer healing and prevention is all about. Not only that, but exercise releases endorphins, our body's natural pain medication, a hormone released in the brain that makes us feel good. Exercise has actually been shown to be just as effective as antidepressants and psychotherapy for treating depression.[26] What cancer patient couldn't benefit from a mood boost?

Exercise also helps your lymphatic system drain toxins from your body. This is very important for me in particular because I want to keep my lymphoma (cancer of the lymph system) from recurring. There are many ways to keep your lymph system happy, which I wrote about in a post on my blog. But what is the lymph system exactly?

According to LiveScience.com, "The lymphatic system is a network of tissues and organs that help rid the body of toxins, waste and other unwanted materials. The primary function of the lymphatic system is to transport lymph, a fluid containing infection-fighting white blood cells, throughout the body. The lymphatic system primarily consists of lymphatic vessels, which are similar to the circulatory system's veins and capillaries. The vessels are connected to lymph nodes, where the lymph is filtered. The tonsils, adenoids, spleen and thymus are all part of the lymphatic system."[27]

One of the best ways to get those toxins and other waste out of your body through your lymph system to be eliminated, especially if you're getting chemo, is to move. Since the lymph system has no pump like your heart, inversions in yoga are particularly good for getting gravity to help pump the lymphatic fluid back up from your extremities to your waste processing plant—the intestines and kidneys. Another great way to get gravity working for you is anything involving bouncing. Jumping on a mini trampoline, also known as rebounding, is one of the best exercises for the lymphatic system. Walking is also great.

Household Cleaners

Common household cleaners are filled with toxic chemicals that we inhale or absorb through our skin. If you have been diagnosed with cancer or want to avoid getting cancer, I highly recommend switching to "green" cleaners. Start reading labels and looking at the chemicals listed. Start doing research into links between these chemicals and cancer. Enormous amounts of chemicals are used in everyday products that are known or suspected carcinogens.

Unfortunately, the FDA currently has a very backward policy (in my opinion) that a chemical has to be shown to cause illness before it will be banned from use. That means that we are all being exposed until we get sick. And then someone has to effectively prove that it was a particular chemical that caused the illness for it to be banned. Even chemicals that are known carcinogens can be put in our cleaners or our food in small "approved" doses with the thought that they won't harm us. However, there is very little research on the cumulative affect of all these small doses nor on the affect of the chemicals on each other. Cancer is on the rise, and in my opinion this "after the fact" policy sure isn't helping. In Europe, they have the opposite policy. If something is suspected of being harmful, it is not allowed until it is shown to be safe. That makes a lot more sense to me.

Personal Care Products

Ever since I was diagnosed with mantle cell lymphoma in August of 2013, I began a quest to rid my home of as many toxins as possible. We had long ago switched to green cleaners, so I decided to ditch plastic as much as possible. Many plastics are made with endocrine disruptors that have been linked to cancer.[28] These chemicals leach into our food with heat, abrasion, or acidity. So I started using glass food storage containers. I found really beautiful clamp closure style jars from France called Le Parfait. And they are exactly that: *parfait*! Using glass is one way to avoid chemical exposure, and I continue to look for ways to limit the toxins in my family's lives.

I also found in my research that chemicals in hair dye have been linked to non-Hodgkins lymphoma, the very cancer I got! And I had been coloring my hair dark brown for nearly fifteen years at that point, since I started getting gray hairs when I was in college. Here's some of what I found out: data from the 1992 National Cancer Institute (NCI)[29] found that women who used permanent hair dyes had a 50 percent higher risk for developing non-Hodgkin's lymphoma and an 80 percent higher risk of multiple myeloma than nonusers, and odds were worse if the hair dye was darker, such as brown and black. A certain chemical called p-Phenylendiamine (PPD) found in virtually all hair dyes, even the "natural" ones, seems to be particularly toxic and has also been linked to bladder cancer.[30]. After I knew this, and my bald posttreatment head started growing hair back in gray, I just couldn't even consider coloring it. It was "au naturel" for me.

The one area I had the hardest time finding chemical-free products in was my personal care products. You know, items such as my body lotion, moisturizer, mascara, shampoo, and deodorant. The "natural" versions of some of these things were not all that effective. I started investigating and found that there is actually no governing body in the United States regulating the personal care industry. So "natural" actually means nothing, and even if a product says it's organic or says it contains no parabens or phthalates, two common chemicals in personal care products that have been linked to cancer,[31] [32] the product might actually have those toxins because no agency is overseeing this in the United States like they do in Europe. This was disconcerting. I tried several brands that seemed pretty good and ethical. They were okay and pretty expensive, and then I found one with which I absolutely fell in love.

Through my friend Heidi, I found Neal's Yard Remedies, an ethical, green, fair-trade, and carbon-neutral company that sells certified organic skin-care products out of the United Kingdom. They've been around for over thirty years and are certified organic by the UK's Soil Association. Neal's Yard Remedies products are certified free of parabens, phthalates, nanoparticles, and any chemical even suspected of being harmful. However, since I became a consultant for them (that's how much I loved the products), in the interest of fairness, I will say that there are other European brands that are certified organic, and I recommend that you find one you like. I think it's important to use a European brand because, as I said earlier, the FDA only bans chemicals that have been shown to make people sick, and in Europe they ban ingredients when they suspect them to be harmful. Since up to 60 percent of what you put on your largest organ, your skin, gets absorbed into your system,[33] I want all of those ingredients to be toxin free.

"Anger is just sad's bodyguard."—Liza Palmer

3

WIN THE MENTAL GAME

Tackling the mental game was a huge task for me. A lot of my identity was wrapped up in being strong and healthy. I believed I was independent, capable, assertive, and could take care of myself. Plus, I was a health coach. Who was I now that I had cancer? I no longer knew—certainly not strong and healthy. I felt like a fraud of a health coach. How does a health coach who is doing "everything right" even get cancer? I desperately wanted to keep my self-image of being strong and healthy. I did not want people thinking otherwise. And I certainly didn't want them feeling sorry for me.

After the shock of the diagnosis wore off, I moved through all the stages of grief. I was grieving the old me—the one who had the naïve notion that I would live into my nineties. In the stages of grief, I went from shock to sadness, and for me that is very often quickly converted to some level of anger: annoyance, pissed off, shouting—all in my behavior arsenal. An angry reaction to a cancer diagnosis is, of course, understandable and perfectly normal. But I've learned over the years that anger, although normal, is not a particularly useful emotion.

I knew that I couldn't dwell on the inevitable, unanswerable anger- and pity-filled question, "Why me?" It was clearly not healthy, and I wanted desperately to be healthy. In fact, I worried that every past angry outburst of mine had fueled the secret cancer cells I didn't know were taking up lodging in my body. I consciously made an effort to stay in the emotion underneath the anger. There is always an underlying emotion to anger, and for me, it is usually sadness.

I moved from "Why me?" to a slightly more constructive version: "How did this happen to me?" I wanted to figure out this thing that I couldn't figure out. As I pondered this, another difficult question came up: "Who am I now with this disease?" I continue to wrestle with these questions. I have theories on the *how* question, although there's really no way to know. I suspect my immune system was weak from eating dairy for years, not knowing that I was allergic and/or that my mental state was not serene, which could have added to my compromised immune system. The second question—"Who am I now?"—is a constant exercise. I am still a health coach and now a cancer survivor. But I'm also a badass cancer warrior. I have strength now that I didn't have before.

Stay Positive and Optimistic

There are studies that show that a positive mental attitude is highly beneficial to healing. For example, it is a fact that people recover better from illnesses and live longer after operations if they have a positive attitude to life, according to research that Professor Madelon Peters is doing at Maastricht University, Netherlands.[34]

Glass half full, seeing the bright side, the silver lining, all of these practices actually boost your immune system and help you live longer. When you're hit with doomsday scenarios such as a cancer diagnosis, this optimistic attitude can be hard to achieve. But kind of like the fear in the last chapter, having negative energy from stress only helps the cancer to survive. And research has well documented how stress has a negative effect on your immune system by diminishing the white blood cell response to viral infected cells and to cancer cells.[35]

But people dwell on the negative. Have you ever noticed how fleeting the happy times are but how we revisit the upsetting times over and over in our minds? It's called "the negative bias." Studies done by John Cacioppo, PhD, then at Ohio State University, now at the University of Chicago, show the brain reacts more strongly to stimuli it deems negative. There is a greater surge in electrical activity. He figures this most likely evolved for a good reason. Our very survival depended on our ability to keep us out of harm's way.[36]

People will be sad for you when they hear the news of your diagnosis. And of course it's a sad, sad situation (to quote Elton John). But honestly, this pity wasn't helpful and bugged me. I knew I was strong and was going to win, so people greeting me with the "I feel so sorry for you" look on their faces was not cool. I didn't want people's pity. I didn't want people feeling sad for me. (Note to friends and family of cancer patients: don't look at them with pity. Your compassion may look like pity; it's tricky.) I wanted them sending positive, strength-building vibes my way. I needed optimism and "of course you'll beat this" attitudes. Gently let people know that you appreciate their concern, but you are strong, and you will win, and you don't want their sadness.

Switch Negatives to Positives

I noticed on a mantle cell Facebook support page that several people were calling their chemo poison. How is poison supposed to do any kind of healing work? Believe me, I knew that the chemical brew I was letting them put into my body was highly toxic. But I couldn't call it poison or even toxic if I was going to keep things positive. So I changed the word I used to "medicine" and always referred to the chemo as "medicine" in my words as well as thoughts (your thoughts are words as well, so make sure all thoughts and spoken words are positive). I went on the Facebook group page and suggested they use the word "medicine" as well.

This kind of subtle mind-set shift is important. You need to be working with your treatment, not against it. I had a few different friends say to me, "It must be hard, being such a natural, organic type of gal, to be putting chemo chemicals into your body." People mean well. But my sarcastic alter ego wanted to reply, "Oh, I can't wait to undo all of the work I've done these past years getting my body healthy inside and out. I can't wait to see what it feels like to have poison coursing through my body!" Really, people? Of course I didn't want to do it, but since it was either chemicals or death, I'm going with the chemicals. Instead, my answer to these well-meaning friends was that I was not thinking of the chemo as chemicals but rather as medicine. I needed the chemo to get well, and that is what medicine does. End of story.

Do Not Believe Negative Statistics

Statistics are not you. You are unique and separate and distinct from the people who participated in whatever study from which they got the statistics. Besides, just because other people had a particular outcome doesn't mean you will. Believe that you are strong and that your body is capable of healing. Never doubt this. "Since statistics apply to groups of people rather than to a single cancer patient, it is hard to know what those numbers mean for any single person," says Karen Hartman, a senior clinical social worker at Memorial Sloan Kettering Cancer Center in Commack, New York. "This [statistics] is one part of understanding your disease that is not always helpful."[37]

People will look up your diagnosis and find out your statistical prognosis and actually want to talk about it, as my brother said his friend did. Kindly inform them that those statistics don't apply to you, and shut that negativity down. Say it with love so they don't feel bad for their insensitivity and quickly change the subject.

I have also heard of doctors who feel the need to let their patients know the "reality of the situation." Well, there is also the reality that people have spontaneous remissions for no apparent reason. Or that people have healed themselves of some cancers with no chemo or radiation by simply changing their lifestyles. There are people who believed they were getting treatment but really were getting a placebo and had improved symptoms.[38] So miracles happen. Even at stage 4. The power of the mind is strong.

That being said, I believe you should absolutely listen to your doctor and follow his or her advice for treatment. What I mean is to be informed by the statistics in making your decisions, but do not believe that the statistics are you. Your body is unique. You can heal.

Laugh Often and Hard!

One of the best ways I found to stay positive was through laughter. I went online and found endless clips of Jimmy Fallon and Ellen DeGeneres on YouTube, because they in particular are comedians whose humor is light, silly, and kind. This was the energy I was looking for. I also exclusively watched comedies on TV or movies. I had a lot of time on my hands, especially in the hospital, and at first tried shows that weren't comedies. I tried to watch a couple of the Netflix series that I had heard were getting good reviews, *House of Cards* and *Orange Is the New Black*. Although they were definitely well done, the content was just too dark. I needed lightness, happiness, and laughter.

Another practice I started on my frequent thirty-minute drives up to Seattle for my at least weekly doctor appointments was to sing at the top of my lungs in the car, which I thought was funny and pushed my "looking good" boundaries. "Roar," by Katy Perry, and "Girl on Fire," by Alicia Keys, were on the radio a lot then and became my anthems, bringing tears to my eyes as I belted out the lyrics. I decided I needed to dance again too, as I used to love to go to clubs in my twenties, so I had my own personal dance parties in the living room. This slightly embarrassed my teenage children, but I didn't care. Basically, I was looking for any and every way I could think of to lighten up! Be goofy. Let go. Laughing really is the best medicine.

One of the things I love about my mother is her ready laugh. She has belly laughs at comics in the newspaper that just get a smile or chuckle out of me. I think I used to be much more like that but have taken on a seriousness with motherhood. It's like this is a really important job, raising these kids, and I need to take it seriously. But I love a good laugh! And I love to make people laugh! I wanted to be more like my mother, and I got to work on lightening up. I'm a work in progress, but it's safe to say I'm making headway.

Dress for Success

One of my practices was to dress up for my doctor appointments. Even when I was at my very weakest and barely able to walk into the examination room, heavily leaning on my husband for support, I had put a hat on my bald head and a scarf to match, washed my face and put on eyeliner, mascara (when I had lashes), and filled in my thinning eyebrows. I put on lipstick or gloss. I also did this any time I left the house and would be seen in public. I felt it was important to put my best self forward. It improved my mood and made me feel less of a patient and more of a normal human being. I feel strongly that putting your best face forward sets you up for success in any event in life. As one nurse said to me in the hospital, "You can't feel pretty and depressed at the same time." Even for my hospital stays, I brought my own camis, cardigans, and yoga pants, and refused to wear their itchy hospital gowns. It boosted my confidence, and it made a difference. I highly recommend it.

Sleep

One of the best ways to win the mental game is to make sure you're rested. Nothing is as stressful as a cancer diagnosis, so it's understandable if it disrupts your sleep. Add to that certain drugs that keep you awake, and if you're in the hospital, sleep is very elusive with all the beeping machines and midnight checking of vitals. But the restful state is when the healing happens in your body. It is imperative to create a ritual to sleep well at night. Make sure to turn off all electronics an hour before you want to sleep. Keep your bedroom absolutely dark. Take a magnesium supplement (if approved by your doctor) or an Epsom salt bath before tucking in to bed. Drinking warm milk (or almond milk for those of us who can't do dairy) has been shown to help get people sleepy. I use ear plugs, and that alone seems to help me fall into a much deeper sleep than without them. I also recommend eye shades and socks if your feet get cold.

Getting a good night of sleep will not only help your body get the healing time it needs, but it will also help keep your mood more on an even keel. This will help you be able to navigate the emotional rollercoaster that is a cancer journey.

"All you need is love."—The Beatles

4

GET SUPPORT

This is possibly the best use of social media there is. One of my dear friends, Kristine, created a superprivate Facebook group for my friends to keep up on news about my cancer diagnosis. It was called MF-ing Cancer: News about Laren. Even though this MF-ing thing was happening to me, I wasn't entirely comfortable being so completely "honest" by using that particular name, not wanting to offend anyone with the implied swear words. I sent out a request for naming suggestions to the 144 members, about half of whom were very active on the page. They pretty much all agreed that the title "nailed it." So I embraced the brash and honest and continued in that vein with all of my posts.

Those seventy-odd friends were an incredible support to me. The other half of the 144 were probably checking in and reading but not posting comments, which was fine. But those people who posted comments became a virtual support team the likes of which I never could have imagined. I'd post news or updates of my health status, questions, thoughts, or concerns, and I would get immediate, like within seconds, words of love and support from these wonderful friends.

The result was that I was present to so much love for me; it was actually really hard to believe. I was so moved by the kind words, the love, and the support. And so touched by the interest and interaction from these people, some of whom I hadn't seen in thirty years. I took them through the whole process with me. I updated frequently about how I was feeling and how I was recovering, what the various decisions I had to make were, and posted pictures of myself like when I got my hair cut off to make into the wig. These Facebook friends were so supportive, sometimes leaving a string of comments fifty people long. It was so helpful in my recovery knowing that people were pulling for me and following my progress.

When I was assigned to the Aqua Team for my stem cell transplant (all transplant patients at SCCA are assigned to a team of doctors and nurses with a color for its name), these Facebook supporters designated themselves as part of my Aqua Team as well. They called themselves Team Aqua and started painting their fingernails and toenails aqua and posting the photos to the Facebook page. This was hilarious and really cracked me up to see all the male and female finger and toe nails with aqua polish.

Pretty soon they were calling me Aqua Girl, and a superhero was born. My friend Heidi created a comic book image of Aqua Girl punching out "Norm," the name I had previously given to my cancer (a *Young Frankenstein* reference, short for Abby Normal). It was funny and badass and wonderful. They stayed with me through all of it, supporting me with immediate comments of support and love. It was amazing.

With my second cancer diagnosis, right on the heels of my recovery from the stem cell transplant, these wonderful people rallied again. Once again they were right by my virtual side. I have kept them updated on the Facebook group page, and they reply with immediate comments of support and love. It was an amazing experience. I have been so grateful.

If you're not a social media type, there are other ways to get support. There are support groups through hospitals; there are church groups; and there is e-mail for friends and family. The point is to not try to go through it alone. It is rough. You need a posse.

Let Love Rule

It has become crystal clear to me through all of this that love is where it's at. I had to work to let the love in from all of these people on social media, popping up out of the cyberworld expressing their love for me. People I hadn't seen in years were sincerely expressing their love and support. It was surprising and touching and a little hard to be with at first. But I needed all the support I could get—all the good juju, prayers, Reiki, positive vibes, and anything else anyone wanted to send me. And why not believe these people when they expressed their love?

I also had people with whom I was close, and we got even closer. It was so heartwarming and was really one of the best results of having a life-altering diagnosis—the knowledge of who is really there for me, who would do anything for me, letting down the barriers and postures and getting down to what is really important, love. That is what makes the world go around.

Sure, the daily annoyances continue to pull me, but I try to keep remembering to let them go. I get triggered and frustrated and get my feelings hurt just like anyone. Maybe more so, honestly, because I'm pretty sensitive, so this continues to be a challenge.

If you want to take this up a notch, I highly recommend distancing yourself from negative people. Surround yourself instead with the friends who have rallied to your side, the ones who fill you up with love and support.

I had an interesting conversation with a doctor friend and fellow breast cancer survivor. She mentioned that the incidence of breast cancer is more common on the left breast than the right. I thought about it and realized that nearly all eight of the women I knew who had had breast cancer in the past ten years or so, were in the left breast. What is up with that? In fact, studies show the left breast is 5 to 10 percent more likely to develop cancer than the right breast. And nobody is exactly sure why this is so.[39]

But my doctor friend had an interesting theory that I found fascinating. What if cancer is more common in the left breast than in the right because the left breast sits right above the heart? What if the emotional energy that our hearts process (from the Indian theory of chakra energy points in our bodies) isn't flowing as it should? We women, who are generally more emotional than men (although men can get breast cancer too), sometimes have trouble letting love in and dealing with all of the intense emotions of life; throw in the heart-wrenching aspects of motherhood, and I could get where my friend was coming from. I know that letting the love in from my friends near and far during my healing process was a big one for me. It was hard to believe and was definitely an area of growth. I know that I haven't been the best at being vulnerable and showing my true feelings. I continue to bring awareness to letting the love in, and, on the flip side, to opening up, being vulnerable, and focusing on showing my love.

"The struggle ends when gratitude begins."—Neale Donald Walsh

5

WRITE IT OUT

Journaling has been shown to be very healing and cathartic. There is increasing evidence that journaling has a positive impact on our well-being. Psychologist and researcher James Pennebaker at the University of Texas at Austin says that regular journaling strengthens the T lymphocytes in the immune system. Pennebaker believes that writing about stressful events helps you come to terms with them, thereby reducing the impact of these stressors on your physical health.[40]

I highly encourage you to write about whatever is going on for you. Get the emotions and events, the frustrations, and the anxiety down on paper. Writing your thoughts on paper has been shown to decrease stress and anxiety as well.[41] It really helps to get the fear, worry, and any thoughts really, out of your head and onto paper. For me, it allows for space to be positive and optimistic. Getting it out of my head also helps me sleep at night.

Gratitude and Forgiveness

One practice that I highly recommend in the journaling department is gratitude journaling. Write or think of at least a few things you're grateful for, with extra credit for finding gratitude for your cancer diagnosis! I wrote a blog post on this called "Thank You Cancer!" The potential for this level of gratitude came to me during a guided Oprah/Deepak Chopra meditation, which I wrote about in part 1. As I mentioned, Oprah opened the meditation by saying, "Having appreciation for whatever shows up in your life actually recalibrates your very vibration." I thought to myself, *Appreciation for whatever shows up in my life? Like this cancer? How in the hell do I have appreciation for cancer showing up in my life? Is that even possible?* I spent the rest of that meditation not really meditating, more like ruminating on this thought. How was I grateful for cancer? I knew that my cancer diagnosis had already given me a huge new appreciation for life. It had brought me amazing amounts of love from my friends far and near. What's bigger than life and love?

What happened for me when I started gratitude journaling is that I found I had a very rich life. I had a sweet, kind, and generous husband who loved me dearly. I had great kids who were healthy and happy. I had a wonderful family and a solid house in which to live. I had dear friends who cared deeply for me. Not to mention I had enough food and clothing. Yes, I had an uncertain future, but right now, my life was full of riches, and I was happy. Gratitude journaling helped me once again stay present and not go down that slippery slope of worrying about the future. No one knows what the future holds. Any of us could die at any moment. What we have is right now, and with gratitude journaling, I was able to see that right now was pretty good.

I recommend doing this every night before you go to sleep. This practice alone can have a huge impact on your outlook. If you do this before bed, studies show you will sleep more soundly because you have more positive thoughts as you drift off to sleep.[42] And as I said earlier, sleep is essential for healing—in fact the restful state is when the body does its healing work.

Start Close and Expand Out

Through gratitude journaling, I found I was moving into the world of forgiveness. This work turned out to be very important and was a huge eye-opener for me. Along with all that I was grateful for, I began journaling about forgiveness. I dug deep. I looked at past resentments. I made lists of grievances from the past. Ugh. It was not pretty.

I took this forgiveness work on as part of the more spiritual side that I wanted to develop. It was very enlightening. I decided I wanted to start with people in my present, not really feeling the need at this point to go too far back into my past. I started with my husband. I don't know how you and your spouse are, but I love my husband dearly, and he also drives me crazy (he knows this). We are both opinionated and stubborn. Sometimes it feels like we rarely agree on anything. There have been many conflicts over the years, some of them with emotional baggage still strapped on tightly.

I found when I started the forgiveness work that I was holding onto years of old resentments. I was right, and he was clearly wrong. As I worked through it on paper, I also found that I was expecting him to be this perfect, ideal husband, the one that I expect only exists in movies—in tune with my needs, empathetic and sensitive, thoughtful and caring. This is not to say that my husband isn't ever thoughtful. But he's a guy! And like every other human, particularly men, he can get wrapped up in his own world and his own needs. He was doing his job as provider, and as long as everyone was alive and well, he could kind of check that off his list. But the nurturing, the connectedness that I craved, was sporadic. After a few pages of journaling, I was able to realize that he was doing the best he could and that I could forgive him for being human and imperfect. We are all imperfect. We are all human. And I saw that it was kind of unfair of me to have such high expectations.

Through writing it all out, I was able to let go of resentments and forgive other people for being human, for being imperfect, and for hurting me. I went on a forgiveness rampage! My new motto was, "I forgive you for being imperfect." I accepted them as they are. People are doing the best they can at any given moment. It's nice to give them the benefit of the doubt and forgive.

During this process and my new motto, I wondered, *Am I expecting everyone to be perfect all the time? Am I horrible to live with?* How hard must it be to never really be measuring up to my high expectations—to be constantly disappointing me on some level! So I then had to turn my motto onto myself and forgive myself for being human and imperfect, and obviously hard to please. That was actually way harder. I'd been a perfectionist for a long time.

Hi, I'm Laren, and I'm a Recovering Perfectionist

I started really looking at this perfectionist standard I had for myself and the others in my life. It wasn't serving me, and it wasn't making things so great for them either. I had always strived to do the best I could do in any given situation. And I think that's a good thing. But when I got to be a wife and mother, that kind of went haywire with needing to be the perfect wife, mother, business owner, housekeeper, cook, and on and on. I was the president of the board for our co-op preschool. Not only did I volunteer in the kids' classrooms, I started a Spanish language after-school club and was chair of the elementary school auction. I went to every soccer, baseball, basketball, and volleyball game. I went to every swim and dive meet and every tennis match. I was an overachiever, but so were all of my friends, so it seemed normal. The trouble was that I was never good enough. I was hard on myself. I didn't have enough time, always felt behind the eight ball, never fully prepared, and definitely never good enough, thinking, *I should have made a healthy dinner to bring to this tennis match!* What I really should have brought was a pitcher of margaritas; honestly, that would have helped. I wasn't fully enjoying the great life I had been living. When had I felt joy? Laughter and silliness seemed to be in short supply while I was seriously trying to be perfect. When I reflected, I saw that the times that I have felt joy were when I was being goofy and laughing with my friends or with my kids. It was when I was singing at the top of my lungs (very imperfectly) in the car. It was when one clever joke led to another, and my friends and I were rolling with tears of laughter—basically the times when I wasn't caring about how I looked or what people thought of me. I saw that I needed more of that.

The cancer diagnosis and treatments actually put this type A perfectionist way of being into the spotlight. I physically couldn't go to every game/meet/match when I was in treatment. Sometimes I was too tired, and sometimes my white blood cell counts were too low, and I wasn't allowed in crowds. But was it really necessary to go to all of them? The kids survived; in fact they didn't seem to even mind all that much. They knew that I cared and that I was with them in spirit.

And on a more fundamental level, it became plainly clear to the world that I wasn't perfect since I had gotten flippin' cancer! How imperfect was that? This was really a hard one to accept, especially in the beginning. It was so public. It was so obvious, especially when I was bald. I got pity from people that I didn't want pity from. My self-image as perfectly strong and capable was really put into question with the cancer diagnosis. I had to learn to let it be okay that I was an imperfect human.

"You should sit in mediation for twenty minutes a day, unless you're too busy; then you should sit for an hour." —Old Zen saying

6

BEING STILL

It's been interesting to hear from women friends in particular who have gotten cancer, how common it is that we are of this same perfectionist, type A, I can take care of myself personality type. What's up with that?

Women are under a lot of pressure in our society to be and do it all. I kept working part-time when I had children. I loved having that time problem-solving with adults. I loved being challenged intellectually. But I also adored my children and wanted them to have the best possible environment in which to flourish.

What I noticed in my conversations with my girlfriends who also got cancer was that we didn't like to ask for help. I did have some help for a few years starting when my son was ten months old until my daughter was two. A wonderful "nanny" Bekah came for two hours a day to take care of the kids so that I could work on my graphic design projects. It was tempting during this free time to do things like go to the grocery store without small children in tow, but I tried to use the time to keep my small business going.

Aside from that help, the child care and running of the household was mostly up to me. My husband worked long hours building his own general contractor business and was tired at the end of the day. He wanted a very traditional arrangement where there was dinner ready when he got home, fridge constantly stocked, laundry done by someone other than him, you get the picture. I was in need of help to get it all done, feeling like I was a whirlwind all day long, juggling too many hats from the minute I woke up in the morning until the minute I crashed exhausted into bed at night. Ted got that I was busy, but he didn't really get why I needed help or why it was hard. "I'd love to spend all day with the kids!" he would say. I loved being with my kids, but at the same time it was very challenging. And on some level, I felt like I should be up to this task; I knew other women who seemed to be doing it all. My mother had done it all—worked, raised four kids, and had gotten two master's degrees in her spare time.

So in order to get more done, I gave up time for myself—the "me-time" that is so restorative and valuable. Interestingly, I did have girlfriends who routinely went on weekend getaways to fill their tanks back up. I looked on in wonder. How had they pulled that off? You know what they were doing? Arranging it! They weren't asking for the time off. They were planning it and arranging it and letting their husbands know when it would be. They were making the requests for help if it was needed. I hadn't had modeling of that sort in my upbringing and was amazed. I did notice, however, that my husband made his self-care a priority. He would let me know when he was going hunting or playing golf. I wasn't doing that.

I suppose maybe I wasn't assertive enough or didn't value my self-worth highly enough. I do know that I was waiting for someone to notice I needed help and then offer it. I asked one girlfriend who was going away to Bainbridge Island for the weekend with her best friend when our kids were in preschool, how her husband felt about her leaving. She said, "Oh he knows I go crazy without a break. When Mama's not happy, ain't nobody happy." It wasn't until I was diagnosed with cancer that I began to realize that my downtime wasn't a luxury; it was a necessity.

Making your own self-care a priority is the key. It is knowing that the time is valuable and needed. I needed a stress management intervention, and I'm not alone. Too much stress is rampant in our society with its hurry-up, more, more, more lifestyle. We are experiencing chronic levels of stress in our lives, and they are on the rise in women in particular. Women are more likely than men to report having a great deal of stress and less likely to exercise or do other self-care practices to alleviate it, according to the American Psychological Association.[43] That's not to say that life isn't also stressful for men. I know my husband is under enormous pressure and feels stress daily. This concerns me as well.

There's an aspect here, though, that I think is interesting and that I think is particularly common in the perfectionist personality type. That is the inability, or maybe it's more the lack of desire, to ask for help. I knew I needed help, but I felt that asking for help meant that I wasn't capable on some level. I was very proud of my capability. In fact, I was so capable that I rarely said no to any request made of me. I took it all on. I could do it all. Well, eventually I got seriously sick. I am not saying that everyone who has high standards and works hard will eventually end up with a life-threatening disease. But stress does factor into the equation.

We all need to make self-care a priority. Take time to chill out, meditate, be in nature, play sports, get a massage, be with friends, and *laugh*! Appreciate life and the beauty of the world in which we live. Slow down, be still, and be present.

Meditation

As one of my new self-care practices, I got back into my meditation routine. I first started learning meditation at the Seattle Insight Meditation Society (SIMS) when I had a rowdy toddler and was also pregnant with my second child. I think I was searching for a way to introduce quiet time into what was becoming a harried life. At SIMS they teach mindfulness meditation, which appealed to me in that it seemed about as simple as it could be. It is just sitting and focusing on your breath. Of course, as anyone can attest who has tried meditation, sitting and focusing on your breath sounds a lot easier than it actually is. Nevertheless, I continued with it, even going on a silent daylong meditation retreat with a girlfriend.

Studies show that meditation has a calming effect on our nervous systems[44] as well as boosting our immune systems.[45] It also helps me feel more centered, and when I got back into a regular practice during my cancer treatment, it gave me an opportunity to tune into my body and visualize it healing. I have noticed that my energy is more serene, and I am less reactive when I meditate regularly.

But meditation is not easy. In fact, most of the time, I feel like I suck at it. I keep doing it, though, because it is a practice, meaning that I need to keep practicing to get better at it. I sit in meditation for about fifteen minutes a day. I was meditating twice a day when I was actively trying to heal my body of cancer. At that time, sometimes I sat for twenty or thirty minutes. I vary my meditations between guided ones with a dharma lesson and quiet ones where I visualize healing in my body, like the one I described with the white light in the first part of this book. Sometimes I have a mantra, but sometimes I don't. The point is to do it. Allow yourself time to sit quietly and focus on the present. Listen to your breathing. Listen to your body. Yes, listen to the birds chirping or to the neighbor's leaf blower. Be present to what is happening right that minute.

What you want to avoid is getting pulled by the thoughts about the neighbor's leaf blower, for example. *How rude of him to be doing that at this time of day! He did that last week too. I'm going to have to have a conversation about this with him. He is really disturbing the peace. Isn't that against the law? Well I shouldn't threaten him with that. Just a nice neighborly conversation* … And so on and so on. Your mind can hitch a ride on a train of thought and be gone before you realize it. When this happens, and it certainly will for everyone, just notice that you are no longer present. You are on the train. Come back to your breathing—back to listening to your breath go in and out. Maybe come back to your mantra if you use one. I have found that I can be repeating my mantra and hitch a ride on the mental train at the same time. I'm talented that way.

Sometimes I use a visualization of putting that thought in a little box to save it for later. I usually do remember these thoughts later and can address them after the meditation. The point of all of this is to have the space between those thoughts lengthen and the time you are truly present to expand. Once you can stay present for long periods of time, you drop into a deeper state of relaxation. I have had this experience of a lengthy deep relaxation only a few times, in which I fell into that gap of no thoughts. I was deeply relaxed. And then I had the thought, *Wow I'm so relaxed. I'm not having any thoughts. This must be what they talk about.* And just like that, I was out of it. Such is meditation. It's a practice.

But studies show that not only does meditation boost the immune system, it aids in concentration, in patience, in problem-solving, and in creativity.[46] Meditation can be a huge benefit to the working world to reduce stress[47] while at the same time increase problem-solving and creativity skills. I'm not saying it's easy, but it is hugely beneficial and is definitely worth your time.

Yoga

Another form of meditation that I love that has the added benefit of including movement is yoga. I first started doing yoga after I had my son sixteen years ago, when I signed up for a postnatal yoga class. It was fun to connect with other new moms and do Down Dog with our babies lying on the mat looking up at us. Unfortunately, my little guy decided to start crawling across the hardwood floors of the studio at five months, way before any of the other babies, and that was the end of the yoga class for me. Nevertheless, I was hooked, and I continued with classes at various studios and then a really wonderful prenatal yoga series with the pregnancy of my daughter. I highly recommend prenatal yoga for any pregnant woman; it helped so much with the birth. I have been a devoted, if sometimes sporadic, yoga practitioner ever since.

There are many forms of yoga, and I encourage you to find the style that best suits you. I've taken classes in Hatha, Vini, Bikram, and Vinyasa Flow, as well as hybrid yoga/pilates classes. Vinyasa is my favorite, but check out different classes and see what you like. What I find meditative about yoga is that, like sitting meditation, the point is to be present to your body and to your breath. It's challenging physically as well as extremely relaxing.

"Acceptance doesn't mean resignation. It means understanding that something is what it is and there's got to be a way through it."—Michael J. Fox

7

PURE ACCEPTANCE AND LETTING GO

A friend of mine has a beautiful house on the beach. She was going away for the weekend shortly after my diagnosis, and knowing I was stressed, she asked me if I would like to meditate in her back yard looking out onto the water. She said she finds it very calming. I told her I would definitely walk down and take her up on that!

When I got there, I had to ask some neighbor kids who were playing in her backyard if they would leave, and they obliged. I sat facing the ocean and closed my eyes. While meditating directly in front of the beautiful Puget Sound, I decided to ask the Universe a question. As I have said earlier, I wasn't brought up with religion and wasn't particularly spiritual and had certainly never attempted to communicate with Spirit/God/Universe whatever you call it. But I had read this in a book and decided to give it a go. I asked, "What does my body need to heal?" Immediately in my head I heard the words "pure acceptance." I had never heard answers in my head before (maybe because I had never asked any questions). Was this for real, or did I make it up myself? I thought this was an odd answer and probably not made up by me since it was not the answer I was expecting. I was expecting something more along the lines of "Get more rest."

What does "pure acceptance" even mean? And why "pure"? Does that mean complete acceptance? Whole acceptance? And who or what was I to accept? Everyone? Or maybe it's everything. I settled on this translation of pure acceptance: accepting everything.

I was intrigued, to say the least. I decided to start with accepting the people in my life as they are. I began the journaling work described in the previous chapter. I found that acceptance and forgiveness are two sides of the same coin. I branched out from there to accept the cancer. This was challenging. This required tears. How the hell do you accept something that is so wrong—something that is just so totally not okay? Journaling really helped me to explore this and get to a place of acceptance—even of the cancer. I discovered that there had been real pluses that had come out of the diagnosis: closer relationships, a new appreciation for life, and the urgency to make my time left on this planet worthwhile. There is a fundamental perspective change that happens with this kind of diagnosis where every day you wake up grateful just to be alive.

I have found that in my treatment journey, this lesson of "pure acceptance" came up over and over. Acceptance started out being about forgiveness, but it grew into also being about letting go of how I wanted things to be. I was not in control of this situation, and there wasn't any way for me to control it. I had to accept how my body took the treatments and how my body recovered. I had to let go of how I thought I should be spending my days. I had to let go of my definition of what I should be doing as a mother and wife, and let it be okay to focus on my healing. I had to accept this really, really sucky event.

But This Sucks!

Accepting this sucky event was and is hard. When I say accept it, I don't mean that you think it's okay or that you're even happy about it. You may find that there are silver linings to your diagnosis, as I did eventually. But what I mean is to not fight it. Accepting means to see that this is what is happening. This is life right now. There is nothing that you can do to change the fact that this is happening right now. If you rail against it, curse it, be angry or sad, be bitter and resentful, that doesn't do anything to change the fact that this is happening in your body right now. Accepting it lets go of all that negative energy and allows for peace of mind, which allows for your body to more effectively heal. Calmness and serenity are the states of being where healing can occur. This is what is happening. This is life right now. I'm not saying this is easy. I went through a lot of sadness and *This is so unfair*! internal conversations. But all of that isn't helpful. It's much better, more useful, to accept; let all of that negative energy go, and get on with the business of healing.

Pure acceptance and its twin, letting go, continue to be the big life lessons of my cancer diagnosis. As a recovering perfectionist, I keep getting opportunities to accept life and let go of my desire to control it. These really are opportunities to see life differently, and to cherish it and the people in it, exactly as they are.

GOING FORWARD

Christmas of 2014, I had recovered from the stem cell transplant and was feeling pretty strong. I was with my parents, siblings, their spouses, and their children at my parents' beach house in Florence, Oregon. There were seventeen of us all together, an every-other-year weeklong gathering tradition we had been doing ever since we started getting married and starting our own families. After the intense treatment and recovery I had been through that year, I was really appreciative of my family and, honestly, just happy to be alive. I was filled with gratitude. One sunny but cold afternoon, I took a walk on the beach by myself. I turned to the ocean and stood there for several minutes, just feeling the cold wind and the sunshine, and tuning in to the rhythm of the waves going in and out. I spoke again to the Universe, this time aloud. I said, "I am so grateful you spared my life," tears welling in my eyes and the words catching in my throat. And in my head, again I heard a reply. It was, "Okay. Now go tell everyone."

Trippy! I hadn't been expecting a reply because I hadn't actually asked a question. I was not used to this hearing from the Universe thing. Again, it didn't sound like something I would have said and, again, I was confused. Tell everyone? Like go tell my family, who were all warm together, up in the house? Or tell *everyone*? Like write a book or something? I decided to do both. I went up to the house and told my family (little did we know that would be the last time our whole family would be together, with the surprising deaths of my brother and father coming before our next gathering), and now I've told you. I am so grateful to be alive, and I hope you have gotten value of some sort from reading my story and the lessons I learned.

The truth is the future is unsure for all of us. No one knows when she will die, although we generally are not present to this concept on a daily basis. Mostly we live on autopilot. We assume or at least hope that we will live to an old age. We might gauge this based on how old our grandparents were when they died or if we have a family history of some sort. Some of us are aware enough to grab life by the horns and live it to the fullest, but most of us don't. We eat what we like to eat, we do what is fun, and we hope for the best. I have friends who revel in their junk food lifestyles and say things like, "Hey, I grew up eating Lucky Charms and Pop Tarts, and I turned out okay." Or I hear stories of a grandpa who drank scotch every night and smoked cigars all day and lived to be one hundred. Who knows how it all works? I don't know what the secret is, since I thought I was doing everything right and still got cancer, twice.

And the weird thing is that most people have mutated cancerous cells floating around in their bodies. Why do some grow into tumors and others not? I think the best we can do is to make sure we keep our immune systems strong, eat foods that are healthy, get lots of sleep, reduce stress, avoid toxic chemicals in our environment and in products we put on our skin, and live a happy, peaceful life full of love and laughter. That's what I plan to do, and I hope to live to be one hundred.

TIPS FOR CANCER PATIENTS AND THEIR LOVED ONES

Other books and blog posts have lots of tips for cancer patients. One that I read that was filled with two hundred pages of really good tips is *Crazy Sexy Cancer Tips*, by Kris Carr, which I highly recommend.

Here are a few more that I didn't read in the books or blog posts that I learned the hard way:

Bring ear plugs and your own clothes for overnight stays in the hospital. You do not have to wear those hospital gowns. And an eye mask. The lights often don't completely dim, and the beeping of the chemo machine goes on *all night*. Be sure to have your friends bring you food.

Take it slow. Have patience with yourself. You may not be as weak as I was, but the best thing to do is move your body every day and try to go a little further than before. Exercise has been shown to help with the effectiveness of chemo as well as lift your mood. And who doesn't need that?

Don't Google your symptoms, diagnosis, prognosis, or survival statistics. Don't Google anything! It's all scary, bad news. Let your doctor explain the disease to you. Ask a lot of questions. If your doctor is the type to give survival statistics, be advised by them, but don't believe them. At least don't believe they apply to you. Because they don't. You are not a statistic. You are an individual, and unique in your body and your body's ability to heal. That being said, if your doctor's explanation leaves you confused, by all means do your own research. Definitely be your own advocate regarding the course of action and alternative therapies that may help.

Find the very best doctor in the world who treats your disease and go to him or her. This may be financially unfeasible, but I recommend getting creative with fund-raising efforts for you to get the very best care possible. This is your life we're talking about.

Another aspect of the care of cancer, particularly in the United States, is finding out what doctors are covered on which insurance policies. Be sure to speak to your insurance company about every person who is treating you and if they are covered. The hospital bills its services separately from the oncologist, who bills separately from the surgeon, who bills separately from the anesthesiologist, who bills separately from the lab tech company. What unfortunately happens while you are recovering from treatment and wanting to focus on your healing is that you now have a pile of medical bills to sort through and try to make sense of. I highly recommend handing this daunting task all over to a trusted friend or family member to take care of for you. And unfortunately, as was the case with my brother's cancer treatment, many insurance companies have a policy of rejecting all claims first with the assumption that you will appeal the rejection. This is a horrible practice that is wrong on so many levels. The last thing anyone going through cancer needs, or even their loved ones who are trying to care for them, is to have to argue with insurance companies in order to not have to pay tens of thousands of dollars in medical bills.

From the "Things No One Tells You" File

Depending on your chemo, you may lose *all* of your hair—as in all of the hair on your body. This is great for the budget (for women) no longer needing bikini waxes but can kind of freak you out if you weren't expecting a prepubescent look "down there." Just warning you. You may lose your eyebrows, and eyelashes too. Here's something no one tells you; your eyelashes grow back all at the same time. Unfortunately, that means they all fall out again at about the same time. This improves with time, but it takes awhile.

Depending on your age, chemotherapy my throw you headfirst into menopause (again, speaking to women here). This happened with me. I was forty-eight and hadn't even had a hot flash yet. I got my period two weeks before my first chemo treatment and then got another the week after it. When I mentioned this irregularity to my doctor, the nurse chimed in with, "Yeah, you probably won't get another one." And that was how they told me I was in menopause. "As in, not another one ever? Am I in menopause then?" I asked. "Some women have them come back, but given your age, probably not," she replied. Gee, thanks for letting me know. I don't think I would have had any kind of ceremony for this major change in a woman's life, but I think it would have been nice to have gotten a heads-up.

For Friends and Loved Ones of Cancer Patients

I get that it is really hard to know what to say or do or how to be with your friend or family member who is going through cancer treatment. Here's my biggest advice: Empathy is what he or she needs. The person does not need your pity or for you to even share that you're sad at the news of the diagnosis. Expressing your sadness may seem like kindness to you, but for the cancer patient it can be a burden. You have unwittingly added to his or her burden because the person may now feel like they need to somehow take care of your sad situation, the sad situation that he or she actually caused for you. What the person needs instead is your support, your strength, and your empathy. Good ways to express empathy are along the lines of, "Oh my God! This is horrible/unbelievable/totally fucked up. I am here for you. Want to go for a walk and talk?" And then listen.

Gifts and cards are nice gestures. If you have struggled to find a good card to send to your friend with cancer or other serious illness, check out the empathy card line from EmilyMcDowell.com. As a cancer survivor herself, she has created cards that are not only beautiful but absolutely exactly what a cancer patient wants in a card from a friend.

I personally loved flowers and plants as gifts because they brightened my mood considerably. However, keep in mind that when the immune system is seriously compromised by chemotherapy, and especially by a stem cell transplant, flowers and plants are not allowed due to potential germs in the soil.

I think getting bath or skin-care products that are free of cancer-causing chemicals make great gifts. As I mentioned in this book, I am a consultant for Neal's Yard Remedies organic skin-care products which are free of cancer-causing chemicals. My website if you're interested, is us.nyrorganic.com/shop/larenwatson.

Many lovely businesses out there understand how difficult it is to live with cancer and go through treatment. One that I heard of, but didn't take advantage of myself, is called Cleaning For A Reason http://www.cleaningforareason.org. They offer free house cleaning for anyone going through cancer treatment so that the patient can focus on his or her healing. They have recruited over twelve thousand maid services in the United States and Canada to donate their time. How great is that?

Lastly, please don't tell your cancer patient friend that there must have been something he or she did to get cancer or some reason he or she got it (maybe he or she was exposed to something in childhood? "Did you live in a toxic area?" Yes, someone actually asked me that. I even had someone say to me, "There is a reason you keep getting it.") From what the experts say, it is a perfect storm of conditions that allows cancer to grow in one person and not in another. A lot of it is random. It is not the patient's fault. Sometimes he or she was doing everything right and still got cancer. Twice.

NOTES

1   *Medlineplus*, "Diet and Cancer," updated 4/25/2015, https://www.nlm. nih.gov/medlineplus/ency/article/002096.htm.

2   *Cancer Treatment and Research*, 1997, "Pesticides and Cancer," http:// www.ncbi.nlm.nih.gov/pubmed/9498903.

3   *Environmental Health Perspectives*, 2006, "Chemical Exposures: Prostate Cancer and Early BPA Exposure," http://www.ncbi.nlm.nih.gov/pmc/ articles/PMC1570083/.

4   *NYR Natural News*, 2013, "The Hair Dye/Cancer Connection," http:// www.nyrnaturalnews.com/article/the-hair-dyecancer-connection/.

5   *Arizona Center for Advanced Medicine*, 2013, "Inflammation: A Common Denominator of Disease" http://arizonaadvancedmedicine.com/ inflammation-a-common-denominator-of-disease/

6   *Yale Journal of Biology and Medicine*, 2006, "Why Cancer and Inflammation?" http://www.ncbi.nlm.nih.gov/pmc/articles/PMC1994795/.

7   *Advances in Nutrition*, 2013, "Health-Promoting Components of Fruits and Vegetables in the Diet," http://www.ncbi.nlm.nih.gov/pmc/articles/ PMC3650511/.

8   *Scientific American*, 2015, "Widely Used Herbicide Linked to Cancer," http:// www.scientificamerican.com/article/widely-used-herbicide-linked-to-cancer.

9   *Immunotherapy*, 2014, "Current advances in T-cell-based cancer immunotherapy," http://www.ncbi.nlm.nih.gov/pmc/articles/PMC4372895/.

10 *Scientific American*, "Another Reason Vitamin D is Important it Gets T Cells Going," http://blogs.scientificamerican.com/observations/another-reason-vitamin-d-is-important-it-gets-t-cells-going.

11 *3 Biotech*, 2012, "Recent developments in mushrooms as anti-cancer therapeutics: a review," http://www.ncbi.nlm.nih.gov/pmc/articles/PMC3339609.

12 *Journal of the American College of Cardiology*, 2008, "Dietary strategies for improving post-prandial glucose, lipids, inflammation, and cardiovascular health," http://www.ncbi.nlm.nih.gov/pubmed/18206731.

13 *Yale Journal of Biology and Medicine*, 2010, "Gain weight by 'going diet?' Artificial sweeteners and the neurobiology of sugar cravings," http://www.ncbi.nlm.nih.gov/pmc/articles/PMC2892765/.

14 National Cancer Institute, 2009, "Artificial Sweeteners and Cancer," http://www.cancer.gov/about-cancer/causes-prevention/risk/diet/artificial-sweeteners-fact-sheet.

15 *Medical Daily*, 2015, "Drinking Too Much Water Can Be Deadly: New Guidelines on Healthy Water Consumption Warns Against the Wrong Amount," http://www.medicaldaily.com/drinking-too-much-water-can-be-deadly-new-guidelines-healthy-water-consumption-warns-340604.

16 *Cancer Treatment and Research*, 2015, "Gut Microbes, Diet, and Cancer," http://www.ncbi.nlm.nih.gov/pmc/articles/PMC4121395/.

17 American Museum of Natural History, 2015, "You're your Microbiome," http://www.amnh.org/explore/science-topics/health-and-our-microbiome/meet-your-microbiome.

18 *Mediators of Inflammation*, 2014, "Role of Cellular Immunity in Cow's Milk Allergy: Pathogenesis, Tolerance Induction, and Beyond," http://www.ncbi.nlm.nih.gov/pmc/articles/PMC4070503/.

19 *British Journal of Nutrition*, 2014, "Exploring the influence of the gut microbiota and probiotics on health: a symposium report," http://www.ncbi.nlm.nih.gov/pmc/articles/PMC4077244/.

20 *Healthy Women*, 2013, "10 Signs You Have a Leaky Gut—and How to Heal It," http://www.healthywomen.org/content/blog-entry/10-signs-you-have-leaky-gut—and-how-heal-it.

21 Foundation for Integrated Medicine, 2007, "Leaky Gut Syndromes: Breaking The Vicious Cycle," http://mdheal.org/leakygut.htm.

22 *Clinical and Experimental Immunology*, 2008, "Allergy and the gastrointestinal system," http://www.ncbi.nlm.nih.gov/pmc/articles/PMC2515351.

23 *Saudi Pharmaceutical Journal*, 2013, "Role of Probiotics in health improvement, infection control and disease treatment and management," http://www.ncbi.nlm.nih.gov/pmc/articles/PMC4421088.

24 National Cancer Institute, 2010, "Guidelines Urge Exercise for Cancer Patients, Survivors," http://www.cancer.gov/about-cancer/treatment/research/exercise-before-after-treatment.

25 *Medline Plus*, 2014, "Exercise and immunity," https://www.nlm.nih.gov/medlineplus/ency/article/007165.htm.

26 *Primary Care Companion Journal of Clinical Psychiatry*, 2004, "The Benefits of Exercise for the Clinically Depressed," http://www.ncbi.nlm.nih.gov/pmc/articles/PMC474733/.

27 *Live Science*, 2015, "Lymphatic System: Facts, Functions & Diseases," http://www.livescience.com/26983-lymphatic-system.html.

28 *Environmental Factor*, 2014, "New study links BPA and prostate cancer in humans," http://www.niehs.nih.gov/news/newsletter/2014/4/science-bpaprostate.

29 *American Journal of Public Health*, 1992, "Use of hair coloring products and the risk of lymphoma, multiple myeloma, and chronic lymphocytic leukemia," http://www.ncbi.nlm.nih.gov/pmc/articles/PMC1694062/.

30 *Toxicology*, 2005, "Lack of evidence for metabolism of p-phenylenediamine by human hepatic cytochrome P450 enzymes," http://www.ncbi.nlm.nih.gov/pubmed/15840428.

31 *Environmental Health Perspectives*, 2010, "Exposure to Phthalates and Breast Cancer Risk in Northern Mexico," http://www.ncbi.nlm.nih.gov/pmc/articles/PMC2854732/.

32 *Journal of Applied Toxicology*, 2013, "Combinations of parabens at concentrations measured in human breast tissue can increase proliferation of MCF-7 human breast cancer cells," http://www.ncbi.nlm.nih.gov/pubmed/23364952.

33 *The News-Herald*, 2013, "Food for Thought: The body absorbs what is put on skin," http://www.thenewsherald.com/articles/2013/06/06/ile_camera/localnews/doc51a67839c14c6578254558.txt.

34 *Maastricht University Webmagazine*, 2008, "The Healing Power of Optimism," http://webmagazine.maastrichtuniversity.nl/index.php/research/mind/item/82-the-healing-power-of-optimism.

[35] 35 *Social Work in Health Care*, 2008, "The mind-body connection: not just a theory anymore," http://www.ncbi.nlm.nih.gov/pubmed/18589562.

[36] *Psychology Today*, 2003, "Our Brain's Negative Bias," https://www.psychologytoday.com/articles/200306/our-brains-negative-bias.

[37] 37 *Webmd*, 2015, "Living Well With Metastatic Breast Cancer," http://www.webmd.com/breast-cancer/features/metastatic-breast-cancer?page=2).

[38] *Cancer*, 2010, "Placebo and nocebo effects in randomized double blind clinical trials of agents for the treatment of fatigue in advanced cancer patients," http://www.ncbi.nlm.nih.gov/pmc/articles/PMC2815077/.

[39] Roche, 2015, "8 Interesting Facts about breast cancer," http://www.roche.com/research_and_development/what_we_are_working_on/oncology/breast_cancer.htm.

[40] Psych Central, 2013, "The Health Benefits of Journaling," http://psychcentral.com/lib/the-health-benefits-of-journaling/.

[41] University of Rochester Medical Center, 2015, "Journaling for Mental Health," https://www.urmc.rochester.edu/encyclopedia/content.aspx?ContentTypeID=1&ContentID=4552.

[42] *Psychology Today*, 2015, "How Gratitude Helps You Sleep at Night, https://www.psychologytoday.com/blog/minding-the-body/201111/how-gratitude-helps-you-sleep-night.

[43] American Psychological Association, 2007, "Gender and Stress," http://www.apa.org/news/press/releases/stress/2010/gender-stress.aspx.

[44] *Neuroreport*, 2000, "Functional brain mapping of the relaxation response and meditation," http://www.ncbi.nlm.nih.gov/pubmed/10841380.

[45] *Psychosomatic Medicine*, 2003, "Alterations in brain and immune function produced by mindfulness meditation," http://www.ncbi.nlm.nih.gov/pubmed/12883106.

[46] *Frontiers in Psychology*, 2014, "Focused attention, open monitoring and loving kindness meditation: effects on attention, conflict monitoring, and creativity—A review," http://www.ncbi.nlm.nih.gov/pubmed/25295025.

[47] *American Journal of Public Health*, 1977, "Daily Relaxation Response Breaks in a Working Population," http://www.ncbi.nlm.nih.gov/pmc/articles/PMC1653745/.

DISCLAIMER

The content contained in this book is for general health information only and is not intended to be a substitute for professional medical advice, diagnosis or treatment.

Readers should not rely exclusively on information provided in this book for their health needs. All specific medical questions should be presented to your own health care provider.

Laren Watson makes no warranties or representations, expressed or implied, as to the accuracy or completeness, timeliness or usefulness of any opinions, advice, services or other information contained or referenced in this book.

This information is based on my personal experience as a health coach and cancer survivor.

Laren Watson encourages you to continue to visit and to be treated by your healthcare professionals; including, without limitation, a physician. Laren Watson is not acting in the capacity of a doctor, licensed dietician-nutritionist, psychologist or other licensed or registered professional. Laren Watson is not providing health care, medical or nutrition therapy services and will not diagnose, treat or cure in any manner whatsoever any disease, condition or other physical or mental ailment of the human body.

The ideas presented herein ARE NOT intended to be medical advice, endorsements or recommendations. However, this book is a practical and useful reference with information to assist. It's always best, and recommended, to consult with your doctor when making any changes to your diet and/or lifestyle.

ABOUT THE AUTHOR

Laren Rusch Watson became passionate about organic food and nutrition when her kids were born, wanting to feed them in the most nutritious way possible. It soon became an obsession and then a career. After 25 years as a graphic designer, in 2010 she decided to go back to school to become a Holistic Health and Nutrition Coach. Little did she know that her hardest work lay ahead when just three years later she was diagnosed with not one, but two aggressive and hard to treat cancers at essentially the same time. Through combining eastern and western approaches, she managed to beat the odds and learn some big lessons about the body, mind and spirit along the way. She lives with her husband of 18 years, her two teenage kids and her loyal dog just outside of Seattle, Washington.

Made in the USA
Las Vegas, NV
24 June 2022

50682489R10080